No president stands higher in the esteem and public consciousness of Americans than John F. Kennedy. The years since Kennedy's death have seen a profusion of writings and media presentations about him. Opinion polls repeatedly confirm his unequalled popularity. How can this phenomenon be explained? What do Americans see in Kennedy that they have found lacking in recent presidents? These questions are of crucial importance to our understanding of American politics and society.

Thomas Brown's *JFK: History of an Image* explores the various images of Kennedy which have emerged over the twenty-five years since his assassination. Beginning his inquiry with the adulatory works produced by Kennedy's admirers and intimates, Brown shows how such Kennedy "hagiography" helped propagate the image of JFK as an idealistic, yet pragmatic hero whose leadership was ideally suited to modern America. Brown also considers the revisionist critique of Kennedy, which reflects a reaction against the outlook of Kennedy's admirers, and discusses the emergence of a more "balanced" view of JFK and his presidency. Finally, Brown suggests the ways in which recent images of Kennedy reflect the disparate needs and objectives of various groups in the United States.

JFK: History of an Image

JFK ∎ History ∎ of an Image

Thomas Brown

Indiana University Press

BLOOMINGTON ∎ INDIANAPOLIS

Manufactured in the United States of America

Library of Congress Cataloging-in-Publication Data
Brown, Thomas, 1954–
   JFK, history of an image.
      Bibliography: p.
   Includes index.
   1. Kennedy, John Fitzgerald, 1917–1963.
2. Presidents—United States—Biography—History and criticism. 3. United States—Politics and government—1961–1963—Historiography. I. Title.
E842.1.B76 1988   973.922'092'4   87-45373
ISBN 0-253-33194-3

1 2 3 4 5 92 91 90 89 88

■ To my mother
　　and
　　the memory of my father

Ihr bringt mit euch die Bilder froher Tage,
Und manche liebe Schatten steigen auf;
Gleich einer alten, halbverklungnen Sage
Kommt erste Lieb und Freundschaft mit herauf;
Der Schmerz wird neu, es wiederholt die Klage
Des Lebens labyrinthisch irren Lauf
Und nennt die Guten, die, um schöne Stunden
Vom Glück getäuscht, vor mir hinweggeschwunden.

Goethe, "Dedication" to *Faust*, lines 9–16

Contents

ACKNOWLEDGMENTS

This work has benefited immeasurably from the constructive advice and suggestions of a reader for Indiana University Press. My sincere and deepest thanks are extended to Kuba Brown for assistance in photocopying the manuscript. No tribute is adequate to describe the many debts I owe the two people honored in the dedication; whatever virtues I (and this work) possess are entirely due to them.

JFK: History of an Image

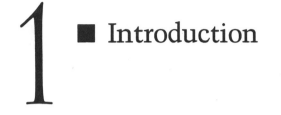

1 ■ Introduction

If there is any enduring monument on the everchanging landscape of contemporary American politics, it is the people's affection and esteem for John F. Kennedy. It has weathered the declining fortunes of the party and policies with which JFK was associated in his lifetime, the bitter controversies provoked by some of the politically active members of his family, and even potentially damaging revelations about Kennedy himself. What makes this phenomenon especially noteworthy is that Kennedy would seem to be unpromising material for a personality cult. His congressional career was largely undistinguished, he won election to the presidency by the barest (and one of the most tainted) of margins, and his major legislative objectives were stymied at the time of his death. Even in foreign policy, where Kennedy did exercise considerable initiative as president, his record is marred by the Bay of Pigs invasion, the collapse of the Vienna conference with Khrushchev, and the escalation of American involvement in Vietnam. It is possible, of course, to explain Kennedy's appeal by reference to his personal attributes—his youth, good looks, glamour, wartime heroism, humor, and ineffable "style." But it is difficult to accept the argument that those qualities alone can account for the public's posthumous glorification of him.

These observations should serve to enforce a commonplace

point: it is the circumstances of Kennedy's death rather than the events of his life that have elevated him to a primary place in the political consciousness of Americans. It is the day of Kennedy's death, not that of his birth, that is annually observed as a benchmark in American history. In large part, Kennedy's murder has taken on retrospective significance because of the period of war, political scandal, and domestic turmoil that followed it. Considered the painful *rite de passage* to a "decade of shocks," it has come to be seen as a national end of innocence, separating an era of optimism and self-confidence from one of pessimism and self-doubt.[1] Because of the rough coincidence of Kennedy's death and the beginning of our collective "time of troubles," some—especially those inclined to conspiratorial explanations of his assassination—have argued that the country's problems are directly attributable to his demise. This argument aside, there is no denying that the Kennedy assassination has come to symbolize a rupture in the collective experience of the American people.

But the feeling that Kennedy's murder was a violent disruption of the national life was not merely an invention after the fact. It was already present in many initial responses to the assassination. Of course, the emotion was a simple one on November 22, 1963, one not yet laden with the historical associations it would eventually acquire. Nevertheless, the assassination was commonly seen as a blow to national self-esteem, an assault on the comforting faith that the United States is a uniquely benign place, exempt from the anguish and tragedy that have accompanied social change elsewhere. The most common first reactions to Kennedy's murder—shock, followed by incomprehension and disbelief—expressed the shared sense that such things simply did not happen *here*.[2] Furthermore, since the president personalized the abstraction of the nation-state, his murder was often felt as an assault on the nation itself. For that reason, the assassination aroused elemental, almost primitive feelings of vulnerability before mysteriously malevolent forces. Tom Wicker wrote of the immediate popular response to Kennedy's murder that the world seemed a "dark and malignant place; the chill of the unknown shivered across the nation." Vance Bourjaily captured some of the emotions awakened by the shooting of the president when he had the hero of his *The Man Who Knew Kennedy* intone: "Into the cave, children. Get back against the wall, while I roll the stone up against the door. Something is moving around out there in the night that makes the earth tremble with its weight." Noting that the overwhelming majority of Americans rejected the notion that the assassination was the work of a single man, the pollster Louis Harris found "a mass suspicion that nameless, vague, unidentified forces were set loose in the country, bent on a course of violence and assassination."[3]

Once it had become clear that the Kennedy murder presaged no general governmental or social breakdown, reactions to it increasingly focused on its *private* aspects. Kennedy had made skillful use of the media of mass communication to promote the appearance of intimacy between himself and the public, and his death was felt as a *personal* loss by millions of Americans, especially those who belonged to groups that were particularly sympathetic to Kennedy. Catholics, Democrats, blacks, and young people often compared his death to that of a close friend or relative and unashamedly cried at news of his demise.[4] The funeral rites, which were witnessed by virtually every mature American within sight of a television set, served to elicit both the private and public aspects of the nation's feelings about Kennedy. The obsequies had grand, almost dynastic features that reinforced the sense that Kennedy's death was a national catastrophe: the continuous stream of visitors filing past the catafalque; the caisson being pulled by a blinkered horse with reversed stirrups; the procession of foreign leaders and domestic dignitaries following the president's body to St. Matthew's Cathedral; the jet planes arching overhead as the caisson reached the graveside at Arlington; and the eternal flame above Kennedy's grave. But the funeral was also experienced at an intensely personal level as well. The presence of all the generations of the Kennedy family—the mother, wife, children, siblings, and in-laws of the fallen president— provided symbols of identification through whom Americans could purge their own emotions of grief, guilt, and shame.[5] Ever since the assassination weekend, Americans in every walk of life and of every political persuasion have felt intensely close personal bonds to the Kennedy family. More relevant here is the enduring contribution of that fateful weekend to the popular perception of JFK: it had humanized him, yet elevated him above the ordinary mass of politicians and public figures.

The catharsis of the funeral completed, Americans clamored for physical artifacts to preserve memories of Kennedy. Coins, medallions, and stamps were struck in his honor.[6] Mementos and knickknacks—many of them in appallingly bad taste—were produced by entrepreneurs to satisfy the demands of a voracious market.[7] Picture books showing JFK at his charming, forceful, and attractive best poured from the presses.[8] Recordings of Kennedy's speeches and musical tributes to his memory enjoyed brisk sales.[9] In the most pervasive evidence of the president's canonization, all sorts of public buildings and facilities—roads, bridges, airports, schools, libraries, and even a New York City ferryboat—were named or rechristened in his honor.[10] All this, of course, was powerful testimony to the continuing hold Kennedy had over the people's affections. Yet the physical tributes to Kennedy were for the most part strangely devoid of substantive content. With a few exceptions, such as the national cultural center in Washington, D.C., the space center in Florida, and the school of government at Harvard, they bore little, if any, direct relation to Kennedy's personal concerns and interests. This was significant in itself; the "shrines" erected to Kennedy's memory arose from vague, inchoate feelings rather than an articulate ideology or world view. They reflected the desire to honor Kennedy as a symbol of national and universal ideals, and their creators tried to avoid ideas or themes that might have partisan uses or implications.[11]

For this reason, only in the *written* sources does one find a significant effort on the part of thoughtful Americans to articulate the nation's sense of what it had lost. This work reflects that fact. Specifically, it considers the prevalent public images of JFK that have emerged since his death as they are reflected in popular and scholarly publications. Some attention is also devoted to unwritten media of expression, such as movies and television programs. The reader should be forewarned that this study has several limitations. For one thing, it discusses only *American* images of JFK. For another, it does not deal at length with the literature on the Kennedy assassination, except insofar as it provides clues to certain images of JFK himself.[12] And this work is not based on everything written about Kennedy, much less everything with incidental references to him. The daunting proportions of Kennediana simply preclude such a comprehensive survey.[13] Rather, the objective here has been to cull the most important sources that have influenced, or been influenced by, the public's perception of JFK.

One additional explanation would seem to be in order. The word "image" is used throughout this work because it is not burdened with the semantic confusions and debates provoked by such terms as "myth" and "legend."[14] What is more, it has been chosen in deference to the common understanding that an "image" is something deliberately created and cultivated for mass consumption.[15] I do not mean to imply that images of JFK have been imposed on a passively receptive public. While a distinctive view of a prominent figure may be fabricated by politicians, publicists, and journalists, the audience they address ultimately determines whether that view embodies its beliefs and values.[16] More important, even the most reflective and self-conscious shapers of the Kennedy image have been influenced by changes in the cultural, political, and social climate of the United States. JFK's presumptive importance in the popular imagination has also meant that Americans have projected upon him their deepest beliefs, hopes, and even fears. The ambiguous and cruelly aborted nature of Kennedy's presidency has also allowed Americans an unusual degree of freedom in interpreting his life and achievements.[17] As the pages below will attempt to show, the various images of Kennedy have been colored by their authors' views on a broad spectrum of subjects—not just Kennedy himself, but the office of the presidency, political power, sexuality, the family, mass culture, and many more. This study therefore aspires to be more than merely a compendium of Kennedy imagery; it attempts, though in admittedly modest fashion and from a limited perspective, to explore shifting American ideals and values in the last quarter century.

2 ■ The Image Created

Keepers of the Flame

The main shapers of the JFK image have been the members of the Kennedy family themselves. They quickly realized after the assassination that the public's posthumous glorification of the late president was a prime political asset and that it was therefore important to help influence the popular perception of him. The family rule of primogeniture made Robert F. Kennedy the heir presumptive to the presidency, and he was not loath to invoke his dead brother's memory—first, in a brief and unsuccessful effort to obtain the vice presidency under Lyndon B. Johnson, then in his run for the Senate seat of Kenneth Keating, next in his career as a senator, and finally in his brutally foreshortened campaign for the Democratic presidential nomination.[1] Since RFK's death, Senator Edward M. Kennedy has kept the torch of JFK's memory burning, as have other members of the Kennedy family.[2]

The Kennedys' zeal to maintain custodianship of the JFK image was most evident in their postassassination dealings with authors connected to the family. Dedicated loyalists from the inner circles of the Kennedy administration, such as Evelyn Lincoln, Arthur M. Schlesinger, Jr., and Theodore C. Sorensen, were extended cooperation in the use of confidential sources when they composed their fond reminiscences of the late president. In return, they agreed to selective censorship by the Kennedys (though in Lincoln's case this did not prove necessary). The Kennedys also extended help to friendly authors and journalists, such as Theodore White. But when writers within the family orbit authored books that did not suit the needs of the Kennedys, their lash was hard. When Maud Shaw, the Kennedy children's governess, wrote her *White House Nannie*, which Jacqueline Kennedy believed contained unduly sensitive information—she particularly objected to the revelation that Shaw had informed Caroline Kennedy of her father's death—the family tried to block its publication. When that failed, they secured Shaw's agreement to drop several offending passages. When Paul "Red" Fay, a member of JFK's "Irish Mafia," included in his *The Pleasure of His Company* several stories that captured some of JFK's all-too-human traits, it was trimmed in half by the Kennedys' pet publishing house, Harper and Row. On further examination of the manuscript, the Kennedys requested substantial additional cuts of potentially embarrassing information. Fay refused, only to find himself excluded from the family circle and his three thousand dollar contribution to the projected Kennedy Memorial Library rejected on the grounds that its acceptance would be "hypocritical."[3]

The Shaw and Fay affairs paled next to the protracted controversy over William Manchester's *Death of a President*. This book was commissioned by the Kennedys as a semiauthorized account of the assassination, and Manchester was extended special privileges to assist in its composition, including that of interviewing the president's widow about her thoughts and feelings on the day of her husband's murder. Unfortunately for the Kennedys, Manchester developed a personal, proprietary interest in the project that clashed with their needs. One problem the Kennedys had with the book was political in nature. Some of its references to President Johnson were hostile in tone, and the manuscript began with a description of a deer hunt at the LBJ ranch that appeared to link the president symbolically to the violence of the assassination. The Kennedys did not object to such passages out of concern for Johnson's feelings, which were hardly an important consideration to them. Rather, they feared that they might complicate Robert Kennedy's already strained relationship with the president and be seen as trying to raise RFK's political stock by lowering that of LBJ. Another problem with Manchester's account was of a personal nature. Jacqueline Kennedy objected to several passages that described some of her thoughts and activities immediately before and after the assassination and was upset by the use of her name in advertisements for serialized installments in *Look*. Manchester finally yielded to the Kennedys' pressure to alter his manuscript and serialized installments and to change some of the financial arrangements pertaining to *The Death of a President* as well. But he did so only after being taken to court by the Kennedys, who in their eagerness to preserve JFK's lofty status with the public ironically diminished their own.[4]

The Kennedys and their acolytes were only the most obvious perpetuators of the JFK image. Lyndon Johnson also made extensive use of the late president's name, both to secure the passage of New Frontier legislation and to help attain election in his own right. It may not be going too far to say that by constantly invoking Kennedy's memory during his first year in office, LBJ helped legitimize his own accession to power by effacing the line of transition between administrations.[5] The Democrats generally found it useful to elevate JFK to the status of a secular saint, whose image was especially useful in attracting the support of younger voters who could not remember the Great Depression and Franklin D. Roosevelt.[6] Catholics had a natural interest in promoting Kennedy as a symbol of their efforts to win acceptance in American society.[7] So, too, did blacks; often critical of Kennedy for timidity when he was alive, civil rights leaders suggested after his death that he was a second Lincoln, whose sacrificial blood had sanctified black rights and aspirations.[8] The creation of the Kennedy image also owed much to authors, journalists, and popular historians, especially those of a liberal Democratic bent.[9] Simply put, the function of such men and women was to interpret the American scene to the public, and they found the Kennedy theme, with its elements of high drama and tragedy, irresistible.

Although the early shapers of the Kennedy image had distinct—and not always identical—purposes in mind, it is not stretching the truth too far to say that a single, reasonably coherent image of JFK emerges from their writings. Since that image is a complex amalgam of diverse ideas, beliefs, and symbols, its various aspects are best discussed separately before they are related to the whole.

Man of Reason

The image of Kennedy as a man of reason was perhaps the most favored one in the immediate aftermath of the assassination. It supplied an easy cliché for newspaper editors and writers who tried to find profound meaning in the president's murder: Kennedy, the embodiment of reason in public life, was the victim of hate and fanaticism. This notion proved especially congenial to liberals for whom the idea that Kennedy was killed by an isolated misfit—and one of vaguely leftist sympathies at that—was neither especially appealing nor meaningful. By blaming Kennedy's murder on an hypostasized mass irrationality, they were able to see a deeper significance in the assassination. In one much-favored argument, Kennedy's murder resulted from a "climate of hate" in Dallas, for which the city's extreme right wing bore primary responsibility.[10] In another, the assassination was seen as the logical outcome of the violent passions bred by extremists of both the Right and Left who were rebelling against the moral ambiguities and complexities of modern society.[11] In yet another argument, Lee Harvey Oswald was the epitome of the alienated and marginal mass man, who expressed his estrangement through ideological extremism and violence.[12] No matter what the specific thesis advanced, the underlying premise was the same: The assassination was not merely the act of a specific man, pursuing definite (and perhaps even rationally understandable) goals; it was an "expression," as John Cogley put it, "of the irrational forces eating their way into American life."[13]

The conception of the assassination as an irrational act acquired additional meaning through reference to some of the attributes of Kennedy himself. Kennedy's calm, reasonable, and unemotional "style" was seen as emblematic of his desire to drain American life of the extreme ideological passions that had claimed his life.[14] In addition, JFK's fondness for books and the company of intellectuals and his appointment of large numbers of Ivy League Ph.D.'s to federal office were hailed as evidence of his concern for the cultivation of intelligence in the nation at large. This receptivity to ideas and intellectuals was played off against the supposed anti-intellectualism of the 1950s, when intellectuals were ostensibly excluded from Washington and the subject of gibes by President Dwight D. Eisenhower and members of his cabinet. Joseph Kraft hence identified Kennedy's "mission" as that of being "an antidote to Eisenhowerism—to identify and meet problems that resisted sentimentality and required brain."[15] Hans Morgenthau similarly praised Kennedy for having "made the intellectual respectable in the public eye, but culture in general as well."[16] Sometimes such assertions confused the interests of intellectuals as a class with the promotion of intellect itself, as in Schlesinger's claim that Kennedy was responsible for reawakening "respect for ideas" in the United States.[17]

While they praised Kennedy for his receptivity to the life of reason, his admirers were eager to dissociate him from abstract, impractical intellectualism. In this regard, they simply repeated claims that had gained currency before the assassination. The unfortunate equation of intellect with ineffectuality had come to be epitomized by Adlai Stevenson, and one of the primary arguments made to intellectuals on Kennedy's behalf in 1960 was that he could surmount the alienation between the world of power and the world of ideas. As Joseph Alsop crudely put it, JFK was "Stevenson with balls."[18] Kennedy's presidency itself was often hailed for having transcended the Stevensonian disseverance between intellect and responsibility.[19] After Kennedy's death, his memorialists debated the issue of whether he should be described as an "intellectual," but they agreed that the label did not apply if it referred to someone who was interested in ideas for their own sake. Kennedy's "intellectual" interests did not extend beyond ideas that could be directly converted into concrete proposals and programs. And although Kennedy was an "ironist" in his perception of the intellectual complexities of the historical process, "irony was never permitted to sever the nerve of action."[20] Sometimes an underlying distrust of, if not contempt for, theoretical intellect (as opposed to "practical" intelligence) showed through the praise of Kennedy as a man of reason. John Cogley, for instance, extolled JFK for having "used" ideas without being "enthralled" by them. Further, Cogley pointed out, Kennedy had often clashed with intellectuals because of their hostility to the "grubby" means necessary to translate ideas into action. But he had accepted the best they had to offer, "while still realizing that in itself intellectuality is not enough for political leadership."[21]

Such encomia to Kennedy as a man of "practical" intelligence were often coupled with tributes to his "pragmatism." Characteristically, Schlesinger tried to inflate this relatively simple notion by associating it with the philosophy of John Dewey and William James.[22] But in common usage, it referred to Kennedy's interest in ideas with practical consequences, his aversion to abstractions, ideologies, and metaphysics, his willingness to experiment and innovate, and his preference for problem solving over theoretical speculation.[23] In this sense, Kennedy's "pragmatism" may be seen as an expression of modern, "progressive" liberalism, whose advocates have prided themselves on their aversion to fixed ideas and a willingness to adapt the state to changing social realities.[24] It can also be seen as an outgrowth of the post–World War II, post-McCarthy disillusionment with ideologies that was fashionable among American intellectuals in the late 1950s and early 1960s.[25] The image of Kennedy as a "pragmatic" man of reason was also related to his admirers' vision of the post–New Deal fate of liberalism. In their view, it had degenerated into an official ideology—a "dogma," in Theodore White's term—that lacked vitality and originality. For this reason, it had become an obstacle to change and required a man like Kennedy, who had no "blueprint" for the future and was unhampered by fixed beliefs and ideologies but responsive to the currents of change in the country.[26] Likewise, John Roche and Schlesinger both celebrated Kennedy's "politics of modernity," which had transcended the conventional divisions between liberals and conservatives and paved the way for the application of revolutionary "new ideas" to government.[27] Roche declared that because of Kennedy, "we stand at the threshold of a new era—an era in which the categories 'liberal' and 'conservative' as we know them may have as much meaning as Whig and Tory."[28]

The implication of all this was that Kennedy's opponents were not merely wrong or misguided, but *irrational*. In their smug identification of Kennedy and his programs with the cause of reason, JFK's admirers at times betrayed a disturbing inclination to equate dissent with unreason. Here, as in many other respects, Schlesinger provides the best evidence. In his view, Kennedy's adversaries shared the common failing that they could not confront the dictates of "reason" because their vision was distorted by delusory myths, dogmas, and ideologies. According to Schlesinger, they included reflexive right-wingers, fearful of the modern world, wedded to the formulae of classical economics, and prone to an apocalyptic view of the cold war; liberals who were unreasoningly attached to various (unspecified) "pieties" and more concerned with gestures and symbols than concrete accomplishments; left-wing extremists infatuated with "utopian" visions of total social transformation; flatulent bureaucrats in the State Department who did not share Kennedy's desire for clear, concise, and crisp responses to world problems; and southern racists and demagogues who refused to acknowledge the irrationality of discrimination and segregation.[29]

Behind this portrayal of Kennedy's opponents it is not difficult to detect special pleading for the interests of the "action intellectuals" and technocrats Kennedy brought to Washington.[30] It is even more apparent in the image of Kennedy himself as the pragmatic man of reason whose freedom from dogmas, myths, and ideologies allowed him to achieve practical mastery of "reality." In this context, the ascription of Kennedy's death to mass fanaticism and irrationality has a larger significance. Not only did it serve as a warning against the dangers of popular ideological passion, but it also lent sanction to the notion that the people should defer to the leadership of elites who were the putative representatives of the force of "reason."[31]

Style

The assertion that Kennedy brought a certain "style" to his office and the life of the nation was perhaps the most common, yet also the most elusive, claim made in his behalf. As described by his admirers, Kennedy's style consisted of a congeries of qualities: coolness, charm, detachment, wit, irony, elegance, lightness, litheness, taste, zest, and a zeal for excellence in all things. The frequent descriptions of Kennedy as an "aristocrat" or an "English Whig" suggest the considerable degree to which those attributes were associated with privilege and wealth; and even in popular parlance, the word "class" (often used in connection with Kennedy) is a term of praise rather than reproach. Few of Kennedy's eulogists were as open in their snobbery as Samuel Eliot Morison, who memorialized Kennedy as a fellow aristocrat; then again, few Americans' blood flowed as blue as Morison's.[32] But the disdain for the average and the commonplace behind the admiration of Kennedy's style is suggested more subtly by Joseph Alsop's saying of Kennedy that "No one could have differed more sharply from the good, average American, who watches television in his off hours, is content if his is a two-car family, and does not mind bulging a bit in middle age."[33]

The frank elitism in the adulation of the Kennedy style becomes understandable against the backdrop of American social thought in the late 1950s and early 1960s. The vogue in liberal intellectual circles, as evidenced by such best sellers as David Riesman's *The Lonely Crowd* and William H. Whyte's *The Organization Man*, was criticism of the United States as a "mass society" suffocating in its own conformity and materialism. Against those lamentable tendencies, the JFK style was praised for affirming "aristocratic" standards of excellence and individuality against the mass man's dull mediocrity and complacent self-satisfaction. John William Ward thus declared that Kennedy's appeal, especially to the young, was that "the world was still an open and plastic world, open to change and renewal, if only one had the courage to resist the tyrannous weight of mass conformity."[34] As Tom Wicker put it, Kennedy was a "Golden Figure" for his devotees, "the proof in himself that America could have learning and urbanity and elegance and wealth and pleasure and beauty—and still have its strength and vigor and idealism."[35] Schlesinger struck a similar note in his praise of Norman Mailer's essay "Superman Comes to the Supermarket" for capturing Kennedy's "existential" quality—his ability to "touch emotions and hopes thwarted by the bland and mechanized society."[36] This theme is perhaps best captured in Schlesinger's rhapsody to Jacqueline Kennedy for representing "all at once not a negation of her country but a possible fulfillment of it, a dream of civilization and beauty, a suggestion that America was not to be trapped forever in the bourgeois ideal."[37]

An analysis of the content and social correlates of the Kennedy style indicates how it supposedly functioned as an antidote to mass conformity and mediocrity. Above all, the Kennedy style was opposed to everything corny, folksy, and sentimental in American life; it achieved definition in contrast to the alleged provincialism and philistinism of the Eisenhower era. Kennedy's admirers repeated *ad nauseam* that their hero would not wear funny hats or Indian headdresses, wave his arms, or kiss babies when he was campaigning.[38] Style also upheld standards of excellence and taste. A chorus of panegyrists sang Kennedy's praises for having elevated the cultural and intellectual life of the nation through his patronage of the arts. Richard Rovere avowed that Kennedy "gave one a sense of caring" about "the whole quality and tone of American life" and maintained that he "proposed to have, in time, an impact on American taste. He proposed to impress upon the country—to make it, if he could, share—his own respect for excellence of various kinds."[39] The Kennedy style was also self-consciously and rather promiscuously cosmopolitan and "sophisticated." In broad strokes, it seems to have embodied the common man's (and woman's) conception of "class." It took its idea of fashion from New York and Paris, its entertainment values from Broadway and Hollywood, and its voguish "new ideas" from the academic cocktail party circuit."[40] The Kennedy style was also critical of established "dogmas" and "pieties," though in a special way. Disburdened of the moral fervor of antiquated ideologies, its characteristic weapons were irreverence, irony, and wit, which poked fun at the disparity between outdated pretensions and modern realities.[41]

The Kennedy style seems to have reflected several major changes in the structure of American politics. Of those, perhaps the most important was the emergence of the "new politics" which appealed directly to an atomized electorate via the media of mass communication. The primary trait of this new political mode was its conversion of the voter into a consumer of political "images" constructed out of the intangibles of character and personality—in a word, of "style."[42] In the audience for the "new politics," the Kennedy style aimed at a special group of voters: the historical generation of relatively young, well-educated urban professionals who emerged as a significant trendsetting force in American society after World War II. This age cohort, which Eric Goldman called the "Metroamericans," shared the values projected by the Kennedy style: they, too, prided themselves on being culturally "sophisticated" and "liberated" from the pieties of the provincial American past. For such people, the Kennedys appear to have provided models of conspicuously desirable conduct—or, in the jargon of a later era, "role models" of the ideal "lifestyle."[43] Of course, few Metroamericans could hope to share directly in the Kennedy style. But that was precisely the point. The satisfactions it gave, like those of the entertainment industry, were almost entirely vicarious—a reprieve from the banality and emptiness of everyday life that allowed its audience to feel that it was participating in a world more exciting and interesting than that of the "square" and "cornball" mass of humanity.[44]

As in the matter of Kennedy's relation to intellect, the praise of Kennedy's style raises some interesting questions about values. Kennedy's admirers made it abundantly clear that as a *personal* matter, his taste was quite commonplace. As Sorensen admitted, Kennedy had no interest in the opera, was bored at the ballet, and fell asleep at classical music concerts. When he was not posturing for the public, he preferred such fare as James Bond novels, Broadway show tunes, romantic ballads, and western action movies. Even so effusive a witness as Richard Rovere confessed that Kennedy's cultivation of the high arts, as in the famous Pablo Casals concert at the White House, arose from the president's vague sense that it was a good thing to do rather than from a genuine appreciation of artistic achievement.[45] Kennedy's conception of "culture," it appears, was distinctly middlebrow: for him, it was little more than a chic commodity and status symbol, certainly not a genuinely enriching aspect of life.[46] In the light of this, it is difficult to resist the conclusion that it was not culture itself, but the benefits it derived from official recognition that Kennedy's admirers valued when they extolled him for his official patronage of the arts. Just as their depiction of Kennedy as a "practical" intellectual betrayed their fear that ideas per se do not matter, so their praise of Kennedy's taste revealed their suspicion that culture needed association with power to remove from it the onus of being effete, trivial, and effeminate.

Finally, as with so many other elements of the Kennedy image, the notion of style was useful by virtue of its very vagueness. Kennedy's eulogists wanted to claim that he had made a great impact on American life but could point to precious little evidence of substantive accomplishments. However, claims that Kennedy had set a new national style proved admirably suited to the inflation of his influence because of their amorphousness. Norman Mailer came forth with the predictable essay full of "existential" claptrap about Kennedy's "revolutionary" effect on American mores and manners.[47] But the exaltation of the effects of Kennedy's style could make even a serious scholar sound silly. Witness the following effusion by Schlesinger, which has all the breathless vacuity of a Hollywood public relation man's press release:

> The combination of self-criticism, wit and ideas made up, I think, a large part of the spirit of the New Frontier. It informed the processes of government, sparkled through evenings at the White House and around town, refreshed and enlivened the world of journalism, stimulated the universities, kindled the hopes of the young and presented the nation with a new conception of itself and its potentialities. From the viewpoint of the fifties, it was almost a subversive conception, irreverent and skeptical, lacking in due respect for established propositions and potentates. Perhaps only a President who was at the same time seen as a war hero, a Roman Catholic, a tough politician and a film star could have infected the nation with so gay and disturbing a spirit. But Kennedy did exactly this with ease and grace; and, in doing so, he taught the country the possibilities of a new national style. If he did not get the results he would have liked at once, he was changing the climate in directions which would, in time, make those results inevitable.[48]

The Inner Kennedy

Style is presumably but the outward manifestation of the inner man. But in Kennedy's case, the deepest recesses of self remained something of a mystery to even those who knew him best. As Schlesinger put it, Kennedy had different "layers" of associates with whom he revealed the different aspects of his multifaceted personality: the witty aristocrat to his friends in "society"; the high-minded statesman to his academic advisers; the hard-nosed pol to his "Irish Mafia"; the dutiful son to his parents; and so on. No one of these roles revealed the totality of the man, whose most salient quality was his complexity.[49]

This ability to suggest profound inner resources was one of Kennedy's prime assets, as it provided the foundation for the exorbitant claims of his infinite (but ultimately unfulfilled) promise. Mailer, as often, began the intellectual fashion here in "Superman Comes to the Supermarket" when he referred to Kennedy's "existential" quality: the "mysterious" air that captivated the public, suggesting that he was "the image of the mirror of its unconscious."[50] Of course, there were hostile interpretations of Kennedy's elusiveness as well. His much-noted "cool" and detachment were often interpreted by ideologues as betokening a lack of deep moral passion or commitment. But to JFK's admirers, these attributes were virtues that prevented him from succumbing to the excesses of extremism, fanaticism, and vanity. Indeed, the composite portrait that emerges from their posthumous tributes bears close resemblance to Max Weber's depiction of the ideal statesman, who combines sober dedication to a "cause" with a saving sense of balance and proportion.[51]

According to Schlesinger and Sorensen, Kennedy's ideal inner balance reflected his early experiences of illness, injury, and pain. While those misfortunes instilled in Kennedy a "hunger for experience" and a "life-affirming zest," they also equipped him with a profound sense of life's limitations. From this combination of emotions emerged an ideally whole and "autonomous" personality that could unflinchingly confront both the promise and the frustrations of the modern world. Kennedy's style, then, was "the triumph, hard-bought and well-earned, of a gallant and collected human being over the anguish of life."[52] His "cool" was an ideal equipoise of feeling, midway between the "heat" of ideological passion and the "cold" of complacent indifference. Kennedy was "cool" not because he lacked conviction or empathy for others but because he "felt too much and had to compose himself for an existence filled with disorder and despair." His favorite quotation, Sorensen noted, was from James Buchan: "He disliked emotion, not because he felt lightly, but because he felt deeply."[53] Similarly, Kennedy's sense of irony did not mean that he failed to take life seriously. Rather, it was because he *did* value life and wanted to see all things—including himself—in their true place and just proportions. One of Kennedy's greatest assets, in the eyes of his devotees, was his ability to laugh at himself—an ability that also showed a self-confidence sadly lacking in most politicians.[54]

Yet there is telltale evidence in the most admiring books on Kennedy that indicates he had an all-too-human frailty: an inordinate concern with his "image." Pierre Salinger, Schlesinger, and Sorensen all conceded that Kennedy was unduly preoccupied—almost to the point of obsession—with how the press and news media presented himself and his administration to the American people. His ill-tempered cancellation of the White House subscription to the *New York Herald-Tribune* was only the best-known sign of Kennedy's prickliness when it came to public criticism. Kennedy was also not above trying to "manage" the news. He attempted to "plant" stories, required the clearance of speeches by high administration officials, sought to prevent the publication of information he deemed sensitive, and tried to induce the *New York Times* to remove David Halberstam for his unfavorable reporting of the situation in Vietnam.[55]

Kennedy's concern about his public image emerges most clearly in "Red" Fay's *The Pleasure of His Company*—which may help explain why the Kennedy family felt so uncomfortable with that book. Fay's Kennedy was a man who fretted constantly over perceived press criticism and was frantically anxious not to be seen (or photographed) golfing before the Democratic convention, lest he be classed with Eisenhower as a duffer-politician.[56] The story that perhaps best captures Kennedy's image consciousness began with Fay asking the president who had painted two canvases on a White House wall. Fay recalled Kennedy's response: "My God, if you have to ask a question like that, do it in a whisper or wait till we get outside. We're trying to give this administration a semblance of class. Renoir and Cézanne just happen to be about the two best-known French Impressionist painters."[57] So much for "style"!

Youth

In the Kennedy image, youth was certainly a vital quality. Kennedy himself was the youngest man elected president, and he depicted his administration in his inaugural address as the expression of "a new generation of leadership." As with the idea of style, the Kennedyite conception of youth was rich with connotative associations: activism, optimism, originality, vigor ("vig-ah"), and the pursuit of excellence. But above all, it implied *idealism*. It was characteristic of the New Frontiersmen that they tried to endow the intellectually vacuous idea of youth with ideological content. According to them, the special perspective of youth was due to its exemption from the moral compromises and conventional wisdom of adult life.[58] Kennedy's admirers almost automatically assumed that youth's impatience with established ideas and institutions invariably manifested itself through progressive causes such as the civil rights movement. Of course, subsequent events have shown that young people have no inherently "progressive" proclivity. Even in Kennedy's own time, the Young Americans for Freedom had as much claim to "idealism" as the Young Democrats. The youthful idealism admired by Kennedy itself assumed diverse forms—the Green Berets as well as the Peace Corps.

To Kennedy's allies and memorialists, the idealism of youth was also inextricably connected with hostility to the routine and commonplace—in a word, to *bureaucracy*. Both the Green Berets and the Peace Corps (and such spinoffs of the Kennedy-inspired poverty program as VISTA) tried to channel the energies of youth outside ordinary governmental channels. JFK's highly personalized approach to the young reached its apogee in the President's Council on Juvenile Delinquency, headed by the quintessential New Frontiersman, David Hackett.[59] The antinomian tendency of the New Frontier was also reflected in its administrative style, which Victor Navasky has described as "informal consultation, anti-bureaucratic, round-the-clock vigils, the crash program, the hasty decision, the quick phone call."[60] Much of the Kennedy administration's air of youthful vitality and vigor was due to the president's reliance on personal loyalists—"we band of brothers"—to cut through red tape. Moreover, Kennedy himself was often praised for infusing the government with new life because of his clashes with "old," entrenched interests in the CIA, FBI, and State Department; his antitheses were J. Edgar

Hoover and the fossils of Foggy Bottom. JFK's "charismatic" leadership style was also central to his intensely *personal* appeal to young people, who could see mirrored in the president some of their own impatience with institutional routine.[61] In this respect, the admiration of young people for JFK in the 1960s bears some similarity to the adulation of a later generation of youth for Ronald Reagan.

Kennedy appealed to the "anti-establishment" bias of the young, but he was only young as politicians go; and Reagan has shown that one need not even be young in that sense to appeal to youth. Why, then, was Kennedy able to meet with a sympathetic response from a generation twenty years his junior? Edwin Guthman suggested a good part of the answer when he described the Kennedy campaign as one of junior officers and enlisted men in revolt against the regime of the chief routineer, Eisenhower. Kennedy's generation, as Guthman pointed out, was shaped by the decisive experience of World War II, which bred in it an "impatience with mediocrity, instincts for action and distrust of convention," along with "a healthy skepticism of the brass." But the years of military service also meant that the ambitions of Kennedy's generation would have to await extra time for fulfillment. By 1960, Kennedy's generation chafed under the leadership of the past, symbolized by the oldest president up to that time. That year, both major parties selected relatively youthful World War II veterans to run for president, but Kennedy appealed more insistently and self-consciously to the aspirations and restlessness of his generation.[62]

JFK interpreted his victory, in part, as a vindication of the spirit of youth. But in fact his own generation's experiences separated it decisively from the sensibilities of many young people born after World War II. Although contemptuous of bureaucracy and governmental inertia, the Kennedy generation's distaste for those things often expressed itself in a war-nurtured cult of "toughness" and masculine self-assertion that in turn often manifested itself in an aggressive foreign policy. By contrast, many members of the generation born and bred in the postwar era were raised in a world of relative security and affluence and were inclined toward values of cooperation, peace, reconciliation, and "love." In his lifetime, JFK did not have to confront this underlying difference between the generations, but Robert Kennedy did. In the 1968 Democratic primaries, Eugene McCarthy appealed to that segment of youth disdainful of the Kennedyite virtues of aggressiveness and toughness. By contrast, Robert Kennedy, for all his praise of youthful idealism, remained more rooted in the values of the older generation. This was not entirely a political drawback for RFK; among other things, it enabled him to compete, as a firm "law and order" man, for the white working-class constituency of George Wallace. And Kennedy retained considerable support among poor and working-class young people, who did not share in the material advantages shared by the McCarthyite youth.[63] But the important point here is that the 1968 campaign showed profound differences of outlook and sensibility among young people, at least within the Democratic party. Those differences would become even more obvious—and more of a problem for the Democrats—in 1972. In this sense, the issues of the late 1960s and the primaries of 1968 helped drive asunder what JFK had helped bring together.

Growth

The idea of growth readily suggested itself as giving a pattern to Kennedy's life. For one thing, it helped connect his life with one of the most universal of human aspirations—for who does not want to believe that the advance of age has the compensatory advantages of increasing maturity and wisdom? In this respect, the posthumous versions of Kennedy's life bear similarities to the archetypal myth of the hero who acquires spiritual insight through suffering and experience.[64] By the same token, the idea of growth helped heighten the pathos of Kennedy's death, as it implied that Kennedy was at the peak of his powers (and presumably still growing) when he was struck down. The image of an ever-growing Kennedy was also wholly consistent with the tenets of "pragmatic" liberalism, as it was the prime virtue of its hero-leader that he struggled to master the forces of change at work in society. Above all, the notion of growth helped make the entirety of Kennedy's life meaningful, for it enabled his admirers to interpret both his failures and successes as contributions to his progressive enlightenment and mastery. In effect, they could have it both ways: they could praise Kennedy's victories unequivocally, yet also excuse his mistakes with the observation that they taught him valuable "lessons." Such "growth" would be the envy of any politician!

The narrative of "growth" conforms to a familiar pattern in most of the major accounts of Kennedy's life. The saga typically begins with Kennedy's childhood experiences of illness, injury, and sibling rivalry that ostensibly challenged him to develop a strong character, prevented him from becoming weak or spoiled, and equipped him with a sensitivity to the misfortunes of those without his privileges. The pattern of growth allegedly continued into Kennedy's early manhood, his heroic exploits in the South Pacific and the deaths of his brother Joe and sister Kathleen further maturing him. According to his biographers, such a process was also evident in JFK's political career. As a congressman, he started out as a loyal adherent of the isolationist views of his father and condemned the internationalist foreign policies of FDR and Truman. But travel abroad and contacts with liberal intellectuals impressed him with the need for American involvements abroad and made him more sympathetic to the aspirations of peoples in the Third World. His illness and surgery during the controversy over the censure of McCarthy forced him to confront the problems of courage and political independence; the fruit of that introspection was *Profiles in Courage*. Kennedy emerged finally as an independent liberal voice through his yeoman work as a member of the Senate Labor Subcommittee's investigation of labor racketeering, which saw him shed his playboy habits and become industrious and hardworking. During the 1960 primary race in West Virginia, his social sympathies were further widened and deepened by firsthand experience of poverty.[65]

The scenario of growth is played out in the accounts of Kennedy's presidency. The Bay of Pigs showed Kennedy's immaturity, cocky self-confidence, and naive trust in the military and intelligence services. As a result of that fiasco, Kennedy acquired a more sober estimate of his abilities and became more skeptical of "expert" advice from the CIA, the Pentagon, and the State Department. This accession of wisdom was reflected in his astute handling of the missile crisis, during which he rejected advice from the Joint Chiefs of Staff in favor of counsel from the informally organized ExCom. From the Vienna conference, Kennedy learned not to underestimate Khrushchev; this "lesson" was reflected in his masterful handling of the Russian premier in the confrontation over the missiles in Cuba. The missile crisis itself contributed to Kennedy's education by shocking him into full awareness of the horrors of nuclear war; this led directly to the test ban treaty. Likewise, southern white resistance to the administration's cautious desegregation policies taught Kennedy the necessity of embracing civil rights as a moral cause; this led to his endorsement of a sweeping civil rights bill. A lagging growth rate and high unemployment rates similarly impressed Kennedy with the need for a revolution in economic policy; hence the administration's support of a sweeping tax program. By the summer of 1963, in Schlesinger's words, Kennedy "was doing at last . . . what he had been reluctant to do before: putting the office of the Presidency on the line at the risk of defeat. He was staking his authority and his re-election on behalf of equal rights, the test ban, planned deficits in economic policy, doing so not without political apprehension but with absolute moral and intellectual resolve."[66] But shortly afterward he was cut down in his prime.

The notion of growth also had the important function of separating Kennedy from the posthumous consequences of his actions. By any objective standard, there was considerable continuity, in both personnel and policy, between the Kennedy and Johnson administrations. But the theme of growth allowed some of Kennedy's admirers to suggest that their hero would have drastically changed the course of government had he lived to serve a second term. By engaging in such speculation, they were guilty of a logical fallacy, that of reifying hypothetical possibilities into concrete realities.[67] But logic sometimes yielded before the felt need to preserve unsullied the historical image of JFK. The portrait of a constantly changing and infinitely adaptable Kennedy also absolved his liberal followers from reconsidering their own responsibility for the problems of the Johnson years; it suggested that those problems were due not to the inadequacy of liberalism itself but to the failings of LBJ's leadership. A later section of this chapter will examine the speculation on what Kennedy would have done in Vietnam, but it was only the most obvious instance of the attempts to adapt the Kennedy record to changing political realities. Once accepted, the idea of growth allowed some of Kennedy's more zealous devotees to indulge in all kinds of wishful thinking. Thus, some Kennedy zealots claimed that a second JFK term would have seen détente with the Soviet Union, the normalization of relations with China and Cuba, a comprehensive test ban, and the beginning of an era of prosperity and racial harmony in the country.[68]

To some proponents of conspiracy theories of the assassination, the notion of a protean, constantly growing Kennedy also helped give meaning to his death. Conspiratorial explanations of the JFK murder have always had an a priori air about them, and no more so than those favored by the president's leftward-leaning admirers. To them, it was

simply unthinkable that Kennedy could have been killed by an isolated misfit of vaguely pro-Communist sympathies. He *must* have
been murdered by insidious right-wing forces that hoped to benefit
from his death. The idea that Johnson himself was personally involved in the assassination also had some cachet among pro-Kennedy leftists, as evidenced by the popularity of Barbara Garson's
egregious play *Macbird!* in chic radical circles and the respectful
hearing accorded Jim Garrison's absurd conspiracy theories by such
professional iconoclasts as Mort Sahl and Dick Gregory.[69]

The image of JFK held by some left-wing conspiracy theorists is
an amalgam of two basic conceptions. One is Kennedy as an "existential" leader, whose estrangement from established manners and
mores naturally allied him with the insurgent forces in American
life. The other is a highly selective and tendentious reading of history. Left-leaning assassinologists claim that at the time of his death,
Kennedy was evolving into an economic radical (his clash with U.S.
Steel), a critic of the cold war (the test ban treaty and promises of a
pullout from Vietnam), and an egalitarian (his embrace of a sweeping
civil rights bill). The individuals or groups assigned responsibility for
the assassination varied with the theory and theorist, but the cast of
favored villains is easily summarized: Texas oil men, angry over
Kennedy's desire to cut their depletion allowance; right-wing "oligarchs" distressed by Kennedy's moves toward détente with the
Russians and his embrace of liberal economic policies; segregation-
ists, disgusted over the civil rights bill; members of the military and
intelligence agencies, angered by Kennedy's failure to heed their
hard-line advice on how to deal with the Communists; and Cuban
exiles, unhappy because of Kennedy's withdrawal of support from
the Bay of Pigs invasion and his moves to normalize relations with
Castro.[70] In the view of the left-leaning conspiracy theorists, then,
the calamity of Kennedy's death was not merely that it cut off his
personal growth but that it thwarted a "lost opportunity" for fundamental change in the United States.

JFK, LBJ, and RFK

In politics, as in other fields, many things—including politicians' reputations—exist largely by comparison. In trying to define more clearly John Kennedy's public image, his admirers often
compared him to Lyndon Johnson and Robert Kennedy. Indeed, it is

not too much to say that those two men were the symbolic antipodes by whom they tried to establish the meaning of JFK's life and legacy.

Lyndon Johnson's relation to the JFK image was bound to be problematic. He was in the uncomfortable position of being Fortinbras to Kennedy's Hamlet and suffered considerably from comparisons to the apotheosized JFK. What is more, his relationship with the living Kennedy had been ambiguous. He had been JFK's main rival for the Democratic presidential nomination in 1960, and the circumstances of his selection for the second spot on the national ticket indicated that he was not Kennedy's favorite choice. What is more, Kennedy had died in Johnson's home state, trying to bring an end to a political feud that Johnson had failed to resolve. Little wonder, then, that many Americans instinctively felt that LBJ was somehow a usurper of the presidency, who shared responsibility for the assassination.[71] The Kennedy family's strained relations with Johnson after JFK's murder compounded his problem of legitimacy. Jacqueline Kennedy rejected the Johnsons' invitations to visit the White House—she did not return there until the presidency of Nixon, who no one would suspect was a Kennedy favorite—while Robert Kennedy quickly emerged as LBJ's chief rival for leadership of the Democratic party.[72] These problems attending the transition from Kennedy to Johnson can be seen as the logical outcome of the Kennedys' reliance on "charismatic" leadership. Since authority under JFK was based on personal closeness to the president rather than on institutional position, it was almost inevitable that the Kennedys and their retinue (the "government-in-exile") should feel that Johnson was the usurper of a position that was not his by right.

The feeling that Johnson's accession represented a dramatic departure from the Kennedy years was highlighted by the contrasting "styles" of the two presidents. Most simply put, LBJ seemed to represent a reversion to the past after the cosmopolitanism and modernity of the Kennedy years. Henry Fairlie and Eric Goldman have ably documented the element of simply snobbery in the common disdain for Johnson; to many of Kennedy's followers, he was a "cornball" and a "slob."[73] He seemed to bring back to national politics the provincial culture that Kennedy had expelled—a culture of backcountry rural accents, funny hats, and exaggerated mannerisms. In his political methods, too, Johnson was a marked contrast to JFK. He practiced with consummate skill the grubby and distasteful arm twisting and logrolling that Kennedy had appeared to regard with disdain. As Tom Wicker wrote, if Kennedy had come to represent for many Americans an idealized image of "the civilization America was destined to produce," Johnson was "the masterpiece, the perfect instrument, of the politics America did produce."[74] Thus Jack Newfield, a moralistic left-wing Kennedyite of Manichean bent, described LBJ as "the Antichrist of the New Politics."[75] That Johnson's techniques met with great success was galling to Kennedy loyalists, for it reminded them that, for all his professed "pragmatism," JFK had not been very effective in his dealings with Congress. For this reason, they often held Johnson's very achievements against him; he was a mere "politician," whose legislative triumphs betokened his deviousness and manipulativeness. Some of Kennedy's image-makers also tried to minimize LBJ's role in securing the passage of legislation. They claimed either that the Kennedy program was well on the way to enactment by the time of the assassination or that the wave of public sympathy after JFK's death assured its success in Congress.[76] The attitude of blacks toward Johnson is indicative of the effectiveness of such claims. While they tend to dismiss Johnson's great help to their cause as self-serving, they memorialize Kennedy as a martyr to their cause. Pictures of Kennedy, not Johnson, grace the walls of many black families, and it is JFK who is recalled in Dick Horder's song "Abraham, Martin, and John" as one of the heroic liberators of black America.

Descriptions of the JFK-LBJ relationship by Kennedy devotees were closely keyed to the political fortunes of Johnson and the needs of the Kennedys. In the early postassassination accounts, which appeared when Johnson was still popular, the emphasis was on harmony and continuity—though only so much as Robert Kennedy's political ambitions could stand. Although the early narratives of Kennedy's choice of Johnson for his running mate indicated that Kennedy's initial offer was propitiatory in nature, they also stressed that JFK had come to consider LBJ a political asset and a fine vice president. Rumors that Kennedy intended to drop Johnson in 1964 were adamantly rejected.[77] Whatever hostility Kennedy's admirers felt toward Johnson tended to be expressed in accounts of the fight for the presidential nomination. Schlesinger, for instance, described a debate at the Democratic convention before the balloting as an encounter between Johnson's "heavy saber strokes" and Kennedy's "urbane and deadly rapier."[78] But in 1968, when it was clearly in the Kennedys' interest to distance themselves from Johnson, Evelyn

Lincoln came forth with the claim that the JFK-LBJ relationship had been marked by increasing enmity and distrust. Lincoln asserted that three days before the assassination, she had asked Kennedy about his choice for a running mate in 1964 and received the following reply: "At this time I am thinking of Governor Terry Sanford of North Carolina. But it will not be Lyndon."[79]

In 1970 Kenneth O'Donnell, a close aide and confidant of Kennedy's, came forth with another "revelation" obviously aimed for political effect. O'Donnell claimed that at the 1960 Democratic convention, Kennedy had taken him aside in a bathroom to explain his reasons for offering the vice presidency to Johnson. According to O'Donnell, JFK had told him that if LBJ had accepted the offer, there was no danger of his becoming president—"Get one thing clear, Kenny, I'm forty-three years old, and I'm the healthiest candidate for President in the country, and I'm not going to die in office." What is more, O'Donnell added, Kennedy had said that the vice presidency "doesn't mean anything," but the Senate majority leadership did, and he preferred the pliable Mike Mansfield rather than the strong-willed Johnson in that post. O'Donnell further alleged that Kennedy had told him that LBJ and Sam Rayburn could "ruin" his chances for the presidency in the upcoming lame-duck session of Congress, so it was important to placate the two Texans.[80] This version of events does not present Kennedy in a pleasant light—it shows him to have been politically calculating and smugly confident of his own indestructibility. More relevant here are the obvious intentions behind the story: to suggest that Kennedy had no high opinion of Johnson's abilities and that he offered the vice presidency to LBJ only for politically expedient reasons, in the expectation that he would probably refuse. No matter whether true or false, O'Donnell's story certainly shows how desperate a Kennedy crony could become to divorce his hero from the presumed mistakes of the Johnson era.

If Johnson was commonly depicted as John Kennedy's link to the politics of the past, Robert Kennedy was often portrayed as his tie to the politics of the future. He was, in the view of many of his admirers—and certainly in his own eyes—the heir apparent to the presidency, destined to fulfill the promise of his older brother. RFK, like JFK, allegedly had his phase of "growth," which was largely compressed into the period between JFK's death and his own, when he ostensibly matured and developed a personality independent of the fallen president's. In the eyes of RFK's admirers (especially those of New Left sympathies), the result of this growth process was a man whose beliefs, ideas, and sensibilities ideally suited him to the turbulent and contentious politics of the middle and late 1960s. It was commonly claimed that in place of JFK's cool, which was appropriate to the banked ideological passions of the early 1960s, RFK substituted emotional intensity and moral fervor. Sorensen summarized this notion when he wrote that whereas JFK could "rationally empathize" with suffering, RFK could "feel it in his bones." Unlike his brother, Robert was also more conspicuously sympathetic to the plight of the downtrodden groups mobilized by the "new politics"—blacks, Indians, migrant workers, and white working-class ethnics. The differences between John and Robert Kennedy are aptly summarized by the modish "new ideas" with which they were associated. In JFK's case, they were counterinsurgency, the "new economics," and "flexible response"; in RFK's, local control, participatory democracy, and the shifting of budgetary priorities from military to domestic spending.[81]

To some, these dissimilarities might suggest that Robert Kennedy actually abandoned the legacy of his murdered brother. But the notion of "growth" allowed his admirers to suggest that he had simply evolved into what JFK would have become in a new intellectual and political climate. RFK himself was not averse to suggesting that he was the personification of JFK's unfulfilled promise. After the assassination, he began to copy JFK's mannerisms and speaking style, learned to speed-read, and self-consciously tried to bring a higher intellectual tone to his speeches with quotations from Aeschylus and Albert Camus. Throughout his journeys at home and abroad, he distributed PT-109 tie clips and made speeches in which he defined the Kennedy contribution to public life as a concern for peaceful democratic progress, coupled with a special sensitivity to the needs of the young.[82] This was not much of a formal political philosophy, but it echoed the rhetorical tonalities of the Kennedy "style."

RFK also implied on occasion that Johnson was *not* the proper legatee of his dead brother. In an interview during his brief pursuit of the vice presidency, he suggested that he would bring "striving and excellence" and an "end to mediocrity" to the Johnson administration—implying, in effect, that low standards prevailed under LBJ.[83] In an especially demagogic speech shortly after his declaration for the Democratic presidential nomination, he condemned the Johnson administration for "calling upon the darker impulses of the American spirit."[84] In another campaign speech, he asserted that LBJ was responsible for violence, drug addiction, and the alienation of youth—thereby implying, by a Kennedyesque inflation of the influence a president can have over the tenor of American life, that Johnson was personally to blame for the major social problems of his presidency.[85] But when LBJ withdrew from the race, RFK no longer had a scapegoat on whom he could place the burden of his accusations. This prompted Eugene McCarthy to quip: "Until now, Bobby has been running as Jack against Lyndon. Now he's going to have to run as himself against Jack." McCarthy apparently meant by this Delphic pronouncement that, with Johnson out of the race, RFK could no longer foster or profit from the delusion that JFK was exempt from responsibility for the travails of the Johnson administration. But RFK took a wiser tack: by dropping most of his references to *both* JFK and LBJ, he was able to put aside the question of his brother's share of responsibility for the problems of the late 1960s and thus avoid direct criticism of the Kennedy legacy.[86]

The Kennedy Achievement

Kennedy's admirers realized that the ultimate reckoning of their hero's place in history would depend on the evaluation of his record in office. No charge stung them more than the one that the Kennedy administration had seen the triumph of style and personality over substance and policy. Schlesinger went so far as to declare that Kennedy had compiled a legislative record "unmatched in some respects since the days of Roosevelt," and he listed some of the measures passed during JFK's tenure in support of that assertion.[87] But his enumeration and similar ones only served to demonstrate that quantity could not make up for a paucity of quality—a sad truth lent particular pertinence by the outpouring of major legislation under LBJ. Consequently, the Kennedy apologists were thrown back on the argument that Kennedy's achievement in office represented, in some broad and intangible but nevertheless real way, a "new departure" in American politics.

The defense of the Kennedy program logically focused on matters of foreign policy, for it was there that Kennedy had concentrated most of his energy and had acted with the greatest freedom, unhampered by congressional opposition. And it was in the realm of foreign policy that Kennedy's memorialists found best typified the hall-marks of his presidency—its activism, flexibility, rationality, prag-matism, openness to new ideas, and growth in wisdom. Here, as elsewhere, they believed JFK had overturned "myths," "pieties," and misconceptions that had hindered American effectiveness during the Eisenhower years. Perhaps most important was his movement away from the doctrine of "massive response," which threatened to make every major-power disagreement into a potential nuclear confronta-tion. In its place, Kennedy substituted "flexible response"—the no-tion that the United States should have the capability of meeting potential threats to world stability by conventional as well as nuclear means. Although this doctrine called for a substantial increase in conventional and nuclear arms, its underlying objective was to pro-mote world order and stability. It was supposed to force the Soviets to recognize that there was a world balance of power in which they could not obtain their objectives through nuclear blackmail but would have to negotiate their differences with the United States. In addition, by giving the country the ability to engage effectively in small-scale, limited conflicts, especially in the underdeveloped world, it would discourage the Soviets from spreading their influence by promoting "wars of liberation."[88]

Although "flexible response" and the attendant arms buildup were keys to Kennedy's foreign policy, they became something of a political embarrassment to the JFK hagiographers. By the late 1960s and early 1970s, they had become associated with Vietnam and an escalating arms race with the Soviet Union, leading so staunch a Kennedyite as Sorensen to admit that they had been mistakes.[89] Kennedy's greater, more enduring contribution to American foreign policy, in his admirers' eyes, was that he broke free of the "dogma" of a dualistic view of the world, in which the United States was seen as the leader of "freedom," pitted against a Communist monolith led by the Soviets. In place of this hoary misconception, which had led American policymakers mistakenly to equate American interests with those of the entire non-Communist world, Kennedy had enun-ciated a policy of "pluralism." The prime virtue of this conception was that it acknowledged the diversity of interests and aspirations at work in the world, including those that did not fit the scheme of a simple polarity between "freedom" and "slavery." For instance, Ken-nedy had acknowledged the legitimate desire of "enlightened" West-ern Europeans for greater unity and independence from the United

States. Hence he had supported Great Britain's entry into the Common Market and promoted closer ties between West Germany and the West—only to be frustrated by the inflexible and outdated nationalism of President Charles de Gaulle.[90]

The new flexibility and openness of American policy, however, were allegedly most in evidence in Kennedy's dealings with the underdeveloped world. He repudiated Dulles's equation of neutralism and immorality, acknowledged the legitimate national aspirations of African and Asian leaders who refused to align with either of the major powers, and supported the creation of a (nominally) neutral government in Laos. What is more, he extended aid to unaligned countries and even to some nations that had expropriated or nationalized American industries. This flexibility and "realism" had another side—Kennedy did not automatically support (as had presidents preceding him and as would presidents following him) authoritarian right-wing regimes simply because they were anti-Communist. In Latin America, Kennedy had in fact repudiated unpopular military governments, such as that of Trujillo in the Dominican Republic. By contrast, he had warmly embraced popular democratic reformers, such as Betancourt of Venezuela and Rivera of El Salvador.[91]

Kennedy's innovative and undogmatic approach was also seen in his strategies for thwarting Communist-inspired or -exploited rebellions in the Third World. One technique, dubbed "counterinsurgency," involved the use of irregular counterguerrilla forces trained in the unique type of conflict required in the underdeveloped world.[92] Another approach depended on the judicious use of foreign aid. Resting on the then fashionable "stages of growth" theory, it proposed to "protect" and rationally direct the process of economic modernization through its social upheavals and thereby mitigate some of the inequities and discontents exploited by the Communists. The unique virtue of this approach was that it adapted to the requirements of local cultures and did not attempt to impose American-style capitalism in countries clearly unsuited to it. It yielded, its planners hoped, countries that were economically stable, independent, self-sufficient—and non-Communist. This optimistic and accommodative idea still survives in some of the more enduring legacies of the New Frontier—the Alliance for Progress, the Peace Corps, and Food for Peace.[93]

The main themes of the positive evaluations of Kennedy also

figure in the portrayal of the major foreign policy crises of his administration. Those crises were all portrayed as contributing to Kennedy's progressive estrangement from outmoded and destructive assumptions inherited from the past. The Bay of Pigs was bewailed universally as a mistake. However, much of the blame for the scheme was shifted away from Kennedy by emphasizing the "bureaucratic momentum" behind it, Kennedy's innate suspicions about it, the "democratic" leaders among the invasion forces, and the CIA's duplicity in expanding the scheme beyond its initial dimensions. Kennedy's defenders also claimed that their hero learned important lessons from the fiasco—to distrust the advice of "experts" and not to trust his own luck.[94]

Kennedy's admirers indignantly rejected the assertion that their man was intimidated by Khrushchev at Vienna. Rather, the confrontation between the two men showed the American's "reasonableness" in seeking a major-power accommodation, whereas the Soviet premier intransigently sought to promote Soviet objectives, especially in Germany. This led, of course, directly to the Berlin crisis. Some of Kennedy's biographers confessed embarrassment, in retrospect, about some of the alarmist aspects of the president's behavior in that episode, particularly the unwitting aid he gave to the air-raid shelter scare. But in their eyes, Kennedy's firm stand on maintaining Allied rights in Germany was ultimately vindicated by the Russians' eventual decision to engage in negotiations.[95]

The missile crisis, of course, figures as the culminating drama of the Kennedy administration. Here, all the distinct virtues of Kennedy found expression. His response to the Russian provocation was judicious, yet firm. On the one hand, he rejected doing nothing, or giving in to the Russian demand for a swap of the American missiles in Turkey; either course would have been yielding to nuclear blackmail, hurt American prestige in the world, and given the Russians increased leverage in Berlin. On the other hand, Kennedy rejected a direct and immediate air strike against the missiles because that would have undermined the United States' moral stature in the world and threatened a direct confrontation with the Russians. Instead, he chose the alternative of a blockade: a restrained yet flexible policy that could be escalated incrementally and allowed the Soviets an "out" without a direct superpower confrontation. In the view of Kennedy's admirers, the wisdom of this response was borne out by the results. Not only were the missiles removed and a clash of the major powers avoided, but in the sobering aftermath of the crisis, both sides awakened to the dangers of brinksmanship and the irrationality of nuclear war and sought an accommodation of their differences through negotiation. The most dramatic and immediate result of this new awareness was a treaty banning above-ground nuclear testing. But others—including a wheat deal with the Russians— foretold a brighter future of ever-widening détente, just as Kennedy was shot down.[96]

Next to Kennedy's pathbreaking initiatives in foreign policy, his defenders placed his bold accomplishments in economic policy. Here, too, he was depicted as a bold innovator and destroyer of antiquated myths and pieties. He was especially praised for giving the lie to the notions, promulgated by Eisenhower, that low unemployment levels necessarily led to inflation, that the government cannot play a significant role in stimulating economic growth, and that recessions are inevitable (and virtually uncontrollable) elements of the business cycle. And he embraced the "New Economics," which proposed to impose rational control over the economy, in accordance with the most enlightened thinking of his time.

Kennedy's defenders, to be certain, conceded that JFK's early economic policies had been anything but bold. He was hampered by his narrow political mandate, disturbed by the low growth rate, and somewhat under the influence of conservative, fiscal-minded advisers such as Secretary of the Treasury Douglas Dillon. Indeed, one of his first moves to stimulate the economy was a classical, "fiscal" one—a readjustment of depreciation allowances to decrease business taxes and encourage investment. But as the economy rebounded and as he came under the sway of such proponents of the "New Economics" as Walter Heller, he moved toward a more activist, countercyclical role in the economy. One sign of this was his adoption of an "incomes policy": the application of wage-price guidelines to assure that high productivity would be coupled with price stability. (Kennedy's famous clash with U.S. Steel arose from a particularly flagrant nonobservance of this policy.) Then, in his commencement speech at Yale University (June 10, 1962), JFK attacked as "myths" some of the beliefs that had impeded a more active government role in the economy—among them, the notions that federal spending had grown relatively bigger since World War II, that deficits created and sustained inflation, and that the national debt had grown out of control. At the same time, he called for rational management of the "techni-

cal" problems of the economy by experts free of "ideological preconceptions." By the autumn of 1962, Kennedy went further, actively
embracing a countercyclical tax cut—"revolutionary" in conventional American economic terms because it proposed to reduce tax
rates while unbalancing the budget, thereby deliberately using a
deficit to stimulate economic growth. Kennedy had also departed
from fiscal orthodoxy by embracing programs to end some of the
structural roots of unemployment, such as through area redevelop-
ment and job retraining. At the time of his death, he was just beginning to consider a large-scale program to combat poverty—more
evidence, in the view of JFK's admirers, of his growing determination
to use the power of government to maximize the productive potential of the country and minimize its waste of human resources.[97]

To the Kennedy hagiographers, the most dramatic evidence of
their protagonist's intellectual and moral growth as president was
his approach to the civil rights movement. They agreed that Kennedy
was always sympathetic with the drive for racial equality; devoid of
racial prejudice himself, he saw fully that discrimination was "divisive," "wasteful," "irrational," and "undemocratic." They indignantly denied that events "forced" his hand. Rather, Kennedy
reached his decision to embrace civil rights "gradually, logically, and
coolly, ultimately involving a dedication of the heart even stronger
than that of the mind." But once Kennedy wholeheartedly "be-
friended" the movement, he acted as the consummate man of reason
he was, to "help guide its torrential currents" into productive channels.[98]

Kennedy's initial attitude toward the civil rights movement as
president was, in Schlesinger's word, "ambivalence." Although sup-
portive of its objectives, he feared that pressing Congress for civil
rights legislation might jeopardize southern Democratic support for
the rest of his legislative program. Moreover, he was disturbed that
the probable obstruction or defeat of civil rights measures might
further alienate and radicalize blacks. Thus Kennedy initially pursued his aims through executive action. By presidential order, he
moved against discrimination in federal employment, and he dramatically increased the number of blacks in high government positions. In addition, the Justice Department, under his brother Robert,
moved forcefully against discrimination. Pressed by the freedom
riders, RFK successfully petitioned the Interstate Commerce Commission for the desegregation of terminals used in interstate bus

travel. The Justice Department also filed numerous suits to promote black voter registration in the South and encouraged civil rights leaders to press voting rights as an issue, because it placed them clearly on the side of law enforcement and was less threatening to whites than desegregation.[99]

These early steps typified Kennedy's rationality and prudence. Unfortunately, they did not reckon with the fierce and violent irrationality of southern prejudice, which was put on full display during the desegregation of the Universities of Alabama and Mississippi and the vicious repression of black demonstrators in Birmingham. Sorensen wrote that to Kennedy, "who lived by reason, the violent response of the Southern mobs and officials brought increased conviction of the rightness of his cause." Furthermore, it fed his anxieties about the rise of "mindless radicalism" among blacks. As a result, Kennedy took steps to "prevent the unsatisfied grievances of an entire race from rending [the social] fabric in two." He dramatically stepped up presidential encouragement of voluntary compliance with federal laws against discrimination and desegregation. He sent to Congress a sweeping civil rights bill that would authorize the attorney general to initiate school desegregation suits, create new programs to encourage fair employment, and empower the federal government to withhold funds from discriminatory programs. Most symbolic, to JFK's admirers, of the president's new sensitivity to black aspirations was his change of attitude toward the dramatic March on Washington called in support of his civil rights bill. After initially opposing the march for fear it might alienate congressmen, he endorsed it (though cautiously) once its leaders reassured him that it would not lay siege to the Capitol. To JFK's devotees, this act, along with Kennedy's substantive encouragement of racial equality, was indicative of his growth to full moral stature as a president dedicated to ridding the country of the irrational and destructive vestiges of the past. Furthermore, in Sorensen's view, Kennedy's forceful actions assured "not only the strength but the dignity" of the civil rights movement, recognizing "not only its full legislative dimensions, but its full moral dimensions."[100]

Vietnam

Kennedy's role in the Vietman War is unsurprisingly the most controversial aspect of his public image and record. Equally unsurprisingly, it is the aspect that has been subjected to the greatest number of revisions by Kennedy's admirers. Such reinterpretations were of course due to the felt need to insulate JFK from the disastrous consequences of the American venture in Southeast Asia. But the Kennedy record in Vietnam was also sufficiently complex and ambiguous to provide revisionists with grounds for changing their views in accordance with changing political realities.

The early family-sanctioned accounts of the Kennedy role in Vietnam are similar in two important respects: they stress the ambivalence of Kennedy's actions, and they wisely avoid reference to LBJ's policies in Southeast Asia. The only major dissent from the Johnson line—and that, *sotto voce*—was Schlesinger's description of the Vietnam conflict as a "civil war."[101] The standard narratives of the administration portray its Vietnam policies as the product of two imperatives. On the one hand, JFK wanted to prevent a Communist takeover in South Vietnam, which he feared might encourage Moscow and Beijing to promote other national "wars of liberation." On the other, he wanted to avoid a large-scale commitment of American land troops, which he feared might become open-ended. The early accounts also portray an administration seriously divided over questions of method and tactics. That split, roughly speaking, was between "hawks," who favored reliance on military measures to preserve South Vietnam's independence, and "doves," who stressed the need for reforms by the Diem regime if it was to enlist broad popular support.[102]

What emerged from those conflicting pressures was a medley of policies in Vietnam. Kennedy repeatedly resisted the military's urgings to send in troops, but he sharply increased the number of American advisers and authorized the use of American helicopters and defoliants in the fighting. At the same time, he pressed for reforms from Diem and promoted "counterinsurgency"—the use of paramilitary antiguerrilla forces (the Green Berets) to encourage popular support for the South Vietnamese government. Kennedy's attempt to manipulate internal Vietnamese affairs reached a peak in his approval (which was quickly withdrawn) of a cable indicating U.S. support for an army coup against Diem. But despite all of Kennedy's efforts, the situation in Vietnam continued to deteriorate, leaving Johnson with a legacy of ambiguous policies and narrowing options. Even Schlesinger admitted that Kennedy "no doubt" realized that "Vietnam was his great failure in foreign policy." Characteristically, however, he added that Kennedy "had never really given it his full attention"—suggesting, in effect, that all Kennedy needed to do to "solve" the problem of Vietnam was to devote more time to it. Schlesinger's concluding comments on Vietnam are both a typical attempt to share the blame for Kennedy's failures with previous administrations and a suggestion that greater emphasis on political approaches would have yielded better results:

> By 1961 choices had already fatally narrowed; but still, if Vietnam had been handled as a political rather than a military problem, if Washington had not listened to General Harkins for so long, if Diem had been subjected to tactful pressure rather than treated with uncritical respect, if a Lodge had gone to Saigon in 1961 instead of a Nolting, if, if, if—and now it was all past, and Diem miserably dead.[103]

Sorensen's verdict on Kennedy's Vietnam policies was also somber. At the time of his death, Kennedy "was simply going to weather it out, a nasty untidy mess to which there was no other acceptable solution." To be sure, his policies in Vietnam had showed "little gain." But the United States had improved its position at least by "not losing"; South Vietnam's independence had been preserved, and North Vietnam and China had been shown that they could not prevail through continued aggressiveness.[104]

Johnson's early conduct of Vietnam policy was astutely designed to emphasize and maximize continuity with the preceding administration's. LBJ retained most of the key Kennedy appointees who had shaped American policy in Southeast Asia. He gave Secretary of Defense Robert S. McNamara an especially prominent role in supervising the war effort during the first year of his administration—so prominent, in fact, that Vietnam was often referred to at the time as "McNamara's war." Johnson also rejected pressure from the military for the insertion of American combat troops and the large-scale bombing of North Vietnam. Even after Johnson began the escalation of U.S. involvement in Vietnam, he continued to defend it as a means to bring about a negotiated settlement. For this reason, "doves" from the Kennedy administration were able to defend the heightened war effort as consistent with the political objectives sought by JFK.[105]

When a debate over Johnson's escalation of the war did emerge among Kennedy loyalists, it was a continuation, for the most part, of the controversy over political versus military approaches. The "doves" in this debate were *not* advocates of complete withdrawal from Vietnam but of greater reliance on counterinsurgency measures. When rumors spread in early 1965 that LBJ was planning to totally withdraw American forces from Vietnam, Robert Kennedy began drafting a speech in opposition to such a move. RFK also refused to join a movement of liberal senators who wanted to withhold funds to support the escalation of the American combat presence in Southeast Asia.[106]

When, in 1966, RFK made his first tepid attack on the administration for not aggressively pursuing the possibility of negotiations, he said that Johnson's major departure from JFK's Vietnam policies was the neglect of counterinsurgency.[107] The reasons for this infatuation with counterinsurgency are not difficult to find. To both Kennedy brothers, counterinsurgency, as personified by the Green Berets, symbolized the romance, élan, and dash of the Kennedy "style." It can be described with little exaggeration as the New Frontier adapted to the conditions of the Third World—idealistic and effectual young men leading the masses along the path to democracy and enlightenment. David Halberstam has described well the connections between the Kennedy "charismatic" ethos and the appeal of counterinsurgency:

> The Kennedy people had taken over from the Eisenhower people, who were flabby and soft; the Kennedy people saw themselves as eggheads, but tough. . . . There was a way somehow that they were going to do this; it was going to be an American decade of intellectualism harnessed to toughness. . . . One of the things it got us into was counter-insurgency; it became quite a fad in Washington. Everybody went around reading Che Guevara and Lin Piao. It really was a sort of romantic period, with a certain naivete to it, and the whole notion of counter-insurgency—these brilliant, young, great physical specimens in their green berets, swinging through the trees, you know, arm over arm, and speaking six languages, including Chinese and Russian, and who had Ph.D's in history and literature, and ate snake meat at night.[108]

Counterinsurgency remained a major focus of the early debate over American policy in Vietnam. In his *To Move a Nation*, Roger Hilsman advocated it as the best response to the Communist onslaught in Vietnam. Hilsman did not advance counterinsurgency as an *alternative* to a military approach but as a possible *supplement* to it. He suggested at one point that the United States might insert troops in Cambodia or Laos to apply pressure on North Vietnam to agree to negotiations. In addition, while Hilsman claimed that Kennedy would have probably supported the neutralization of all of Indochina as the result of negotiations, he also stated that such a settlement would be possible only after the Communist drive in Vietnam had been "blunted" militarily.[109] Schlesinger's *The Bitter Heritage* restated the conventional "dove" line on Vietnam. He expressly rejected the unilateral withdrawal of American troops from Vietnam, though he did call for negotiations with North Vietnam and the Vietcong. His major criticism of Johnson was that he had neglected counterinsurgency and other "political" means to reform and strengthen the South Vietnamese government.[110]

Most early public discussions of Vietnam avoided asking "what might have been" had Kennedy not been murdered. But that question seems to have been a frequent subject of debate in certain academic and governmental circles. Chester Cooper reported that it often became a hot topic at Washington cocktail parties when visitors from Cambridge or New York were present.[111] Some hypothetical discussions of what JFK would have done in Vietnam did find their way into print. Invariably, their arguments were based on the intangibles of personality and "style." In an article in *Harper's*, Clayton Fritchey traced the roots of Johnson's failures in Vietnam to an un-Kennedyesque inability to learn and grow in office. According to Fritchey, Kennedy had emphasized the political aspect of the American response to the conflict in South Vietnam and "had no intention" of getting the United States involved in a land war in Asia. Kennedy "underwent a transformation in office"; he had "learned" that American policy must accommodate itself to new realities, including the breakup of the Communist monolith. For these reasons, Fritchey maintained, Kennedy would never have plunged the United States into a massive, open-ended commitment in Vietnam.[112] Tom Wicker advanced a similar argument, premised on Kennedy's ostensible "growth." He argued that Kennedy would have been less inclined than Johnson to a military solution in Vietnam for two basic reasons: he had learned to distrust the advice of experts in the Bay of Pigs crisis, and he would have had more flexibility of action due to the great prestige he had won in the missile crisis.[113]

But of course it was Robert Kennedy who played the most important role in shaping the public's perceptions of the differences in Vietnam policy between the Kennedy and Johnson administrations. By his own admission, RFK's feelings on the matter were complicated. He and his brother *had* played a large part in expanding the

American role in Vietnam; furthermore, JFK had chosen LBJ as his running mate and thus bore indirect responsibility for Johnson's accession to the presidency.[114] In 1967 RFK did seek to make a sharp distinction between the two presidents' actions in Vietnam. In a rambling, almost incoherent monologue on a television interview show, he criticized LBJ for abandoning the objective of making South Vietnam more self-reliant. He also condemned the administration for arguing that it was taking a strong stand in Southeast Asia to prevent an eventual Communist attack on the United States.[115] But even after he made his sharp break with Johnson and began his presidential candidacy, RFK remained leery of attributing blame for the Vietnam calamity. When asked about his brother's and his own roles in Vietnam policy, his response was that mistakes may have been made in the past, for which he and JFK shared responsibility. But he hastened to add that past errors were no excuse for their "perpetuation."[116] This answer was both politically astute and filiopietistic, as it allowed RFK to divorce himself from his beloved brother without seeming to dishonor his memory.

To his credit, Robert Kennedy steered clear of the question of what his brother might have done in Vietnam. But in the late 1960s, as it became clearer that the war in Southeast Asia was a disaster for the United States, some of JFK's admirers forged ahead where RFK had feared to tread. Norman Mailer, for instance, stated flatly that it had been Kennedy's "unstated policy" in Vietnam to "lose quietly" and "get out"—though how, if this policy was unstated, Mailer knew about it, he did not say.[117] Henry Brandon declined to offer a definitive answer to the hypothetical question but suggested that Kennedy would at least have been more cautious than Johnson. Brandon's reasoning was that at the time of his death, JFK had begun to question some of the "fundamental assumptions" underlying American involvement in Vietnam. Brandon claimed Kennedy was also more "temperate" and "pragmatic," as well as less "prestige-conscious" than LBJ.[118] In *The Kennedy Legacy*, Sorensen advanced an argument similar to Tom Wicker's. He asserted that Kennedy would have probably avoided increasing the United States' military role in Vietnam because the Berlin and Cuban missile crises had taught him that arms buildups caused only equivalent counterescalations.[119]

Kenneth O'Donnell supplied additional fodder for such speculation in 1970. O'Donnell's story followed, in broad outline, the scenario of "growth." It claimed that Kennedy had first developed serious doubts about the American involvement in 1961, when de Gaulle and General Douglas MacArthur warned him of the danger of becoming trapped in a land war in Asia. But Kennedy had not devoted much attention to Vietnam in 1961–1962, O'Donnell asserted, because it had been "overshadowed" by the crises in Berlin and Cuba. Worse still, Kennedy had been compelled to send more advisers to South Vietnam in 1962 because his defeat of Khrushchev in the missile crisis had hurt Russian prestige in the Communist world, increasing the threat of a Chinese move on South Vietnam. But shortly after this enlargement of the American role, Senator Mike Mansfield warned Kennedy that the United States was in danger of dominating the conflict and advised the president to pull out. O'Donnell claimed that Kennedy became angry at this line of argument but added that the president later said that he agreed with Mansfield's reasoning. Mansfield reiterated his argument at a White House congressional briefing in the spring of 1963, again to Kennedy's professed consternation. But this time the president took Mansfield and O'Donnell into a separate office for a private meeting. According to O'Donnell, Kennedy told Mansfield that he agreed that the United States should withdraw totally from Vietnam but that he would hold back the announcement of his decision until after his reelection because he feared a "wild conservative outcry." O'Donnell maintained that after Mansfield left the office, Kennedy added: "In 1965, I'll be damned everywhere as a Communist appeaser. But I don't care. If I tried to pull out completely now, we would have another Joe McCarthy red scare on our hands, but I can do it after I'm reelected. So we had better make damned sure that I *am* reelected." O'Donnell recalled that on another occasion, Kennedy was asked how he would manage a U.S. withdrawal from Vietnam without damage to American prestige. Kennedy rejoined: "Easy. Put a government in there that will ask us to leave."[120]

One need not reject this story out of hand—and Mansfield has confirmed *his* part of it—to doubt that it was a firm statement of Kennedy's intentions in Vietnam.[121] Like many politicians, JFK was inclined to tell people what they wanted to hear—and also not averse to changing his mind. What is more, like O'Donnell's version of the choice of LBJ for the vice presidential nomination, the story does not reflect much credit on Kennedy. It shows him to have been cynically manipulative with young men's lives and craven before the liberal bogey of right-wing reaction; unsurprisingly, Lyndon Johnson used the same reasons Kennedy invoked in O'Donnell's story to justify *escalation* of American involvement in Vietnam. But such considerations seem to be beside the point for Kennedy devotees who have embraced the O'Donnell story as gospel truth.[122] The important thing was that JFK be absolved of responsibility for the Vietnam debacle; when the need for exculpation is so urgent, no obstacles— including morality and the truth—should stand in the way.

A Hero for His Times

The temptation to find legendary and mythical resonances in Kennedy's life and death was too strong for some to resist. Shortly after the assassination, Gerald Johnson wrote that JFK had already joined the ranks of youthful heroes who would remain forever young in the popular imagination.[123] William G. Carleton expressed a similar view in an article published the year after JFK's slaying. As he saw it, Kennedy was well on the way to becoming a "folk hero," "one who leaves behind him an over-all impression of élan, style, beauty, grace, gaiety, gallantry, bold and light-hearted adventure, valor—mingled in one way or another with the frail, the fey, the heedless, the mystic, the tragic." Kennedy's heroic aspects were dramatized, Carleton observed, by the circumstances of his death, which had in it "the touch of religious epic, of man pitted against fate." Kennedy was "surely . . . one favored by the gods," but then, "in the fullness of his strength, he was cut down in a flash. History has no more dramatic demonstration of the everlasting insecurity of the human condition."[124]

In Manchester's *Death of a President*, Kennedy is symbolically elevated into the pantheon of life-affirming heroes cut down by the life-denying forces of darkness, but whose sacrificial blood revitalizes their culture. In Manchester's view, Kennedy and Oswald were the modern correlatives of Arthur and Modred, Roland and Ganelon, Balder and Loki, Siegfried and Hagen, and Osiris and Set.[125] Employing Lord Raglan's paradigmatic interpretation of the classical hero, Marshall Fishwick has given us the fullest version of the Kennedy-as-hero mythos:

> His father was called to a royal court (as Ambassador to the Court of Saint James) and the son was educated by (presumably) wise men (at Harvard). Then he went off to fight an evil dragon (the Japanese navy) and after a bloody fracas (PT 109) triumphed and returned to marry the beautiful

princess (Jackie). Having inherited his father's kingdom (politics) he fought and defeated a second contender (Nixon) before taking over as ruler (President). For a time he suddenly lost favor (the Bay of Pigs crisis), tried to rally his people, and died a sudden and mysterious death (did Oswald really shoot Kennedy?). Amidst great mourning (the first world-wide television funeral) he was buried on a sacred hillside (Arlington). Now he has many shrines (a cultural center, airport, library, and a space launching site).[126]

Of course, the legend most closely connected to the Kennedy image is that of Camelot. The origins of the association may be found in Jacqueline Kennedy's tearful confession to Theodore White shortly after the assassination:

> "At night, before we'd go to sleep, Jack liked to play some records; and the song he loved most came at the very end of this record. The lines he loved to hear were: *Don't let it be forgot, that once there was a spot, for one brief shining moment that was known as Camelot.*
> She wanted to make sure that the point came clear and went on: "There'll be great Presidents again—and the Johnsons are wonderful, they've been wonderful to me—but there'll never be another Camelot again."[127]

Camelot, like any symbol, serves to congeal diverse ideas and emotions in a single image. As Jacqueline Kennedy used it, Camelot suggested that the Kennedy presidency was a special time, exempt from the boredom and routine of "mere" politics, glittering with glamour, full of benevolence, and presided over by a handsome king with his beautiful queen.[128] Loyal Kennedy followers have typically denounced or ridiculed the Camelot symbol as either unduly senti-mental or simply unreal.[129] But this has not prevented the Kennedys from reaping the benefits of its evocation of images of elegance, power, and virtue combined. Many people seem to be infatuated with it. When Robert Kennedy and Edward Kennedy made their runs for the Democratic presidential nomination, signs invoking Camelot dotted their crowds. While RFK contemplated whether he should oppose LBJ in 1968, an admirer in Evanston, Illinois wrote: "Please reconvene the round table. We want Camelot again."[130]

It is possible to find deep latent meanings in Camelot. The image is especially interesting because the United States was conceived in the revolt of a simple, virtuous "Country" against the decadence and grandeur of the English "Court."[131] Camelot, then, may be taken as a metaphor of how the New Frontiersmen conceived of themselves: as a cultured, cosmopolitan elite who would lead the United States away from its provincial past and prepare it for the tasks of empire.[132] The use of a monarchical symbol to describe the government of a republic can be seen as the natural outcome of the Kennedys' tendency toward centralized, personalized authority based on "charisma"—of what Schlesinger, of all people, would later condemn as the "imperial presidency." Furthermore, Camelot lends credence to the frequently repeated charge that the Kennedys feel they have a dynastic right to the presidency. But in the end, the Camelot image seems more banal and fake than dangerous; it promises fantasy rather than fulfillment. It is only appropriate, then, that it was not inspired by the genuine legend of Camelot, but by the insipidly sentimentalized version in a Broadway musical.

Despite attempts to elevate the JFK image into a supermundane realm, its content and appeal can be explained quite easily. As indicated above, its ideal of "pragmatic," managerial liberalism may be traced to the disillusionment of American intellectuals with sweeping ideologies in the post–World War II, post-McCarthy era. Similarly, the conception of Kennedy as the ultimate "realistic" intellectual, with its concomitant association of intellect with power and privilege, can be seen as a reflection of the self-image of power-oriented intellectuals and technocrats who saw the Kennedy administration as the apogee of their influence over American life. The infatuation with Kennedy's "style" can be attributed to the infection of American politics by consumer culture and its cult of "celebrity." And the obsession with Kennedy's youthfulness and vitality can be interpreted as a natural outgrowth of the high proportion of young people in the U.S. population in the 1960s due to the postwar "baby boom."

Another line of argument suggests that the content of the Kennedy image was connected to certain gross demographic trends in American society. In this conception, JFK served as a positive symbol for insurgent groups in the United States striving to find political expression. To urbanites restive under centuries of rural domination, Kennedy was the ultimate cosmopolite; to the post–World War II generation, chafing under the weight of the past, he represented a new generation of leadership; to newly assertive racial and ethnic groups, he was a symbol of as yet unfulfilled opportunities; and to the college-educated and "sophisticated," he epitomized the hope that intellect and vision could transform American politics from its obeisance to cornball ritual and bureaucratic routine. Considered in the light of this argument, there would seem to be some historical sanction for Theodore White's description of Kennedy as the "gatekeeper" who symbolically broke the hold of rural WASP culture on American political life. White's emphasis was on JFK as precipitant rather than as deliberate agent. But for him, this did not detract from Kennedy's central role in modern American history:

> Historically, he was a gatekeeper. He unlatched the door, and through the door marched not only Catholics, but blacks, and Jews, and ethnics, women, youth, academics, newspersons and an entirely new breed of young politicians who did not think of themselves as politicians—all demanding their share of the action and the power in what is now called participatory democracy.[133]

These remarks help place in historical perspective the posthumous canonization of Kennedy by minority groups in American society. For by elevating Kennedy's death into a blood-sacrifice for the nation's sins of bigotry and reaction, they were making their own claims of sympathy and respectability on the country.

At its most elemental level, the Kennedy image is that of unfulfilled promise. This is not merely because of the personal calamity of a young man cut down in the prime of manhood, but also because Kennedy's murder has come to symbolize the nation's thwarted hopes. In this respect, Kennedy's posthumous image has benefited from his place in history. Not only was Kennedy president in a period of relative prosperity, peace, and social stability; more important, he is associated in the minds of Americans with their highest ideals and dreams of power, but not with the costs of change. In the popular view, Kennedy is connected with the high hopes and optimism of the early movement for black rights, when it espoused traditional American ideals of equal opportunity, fair play, and legal due process. But Kennedy has escaped responsibility for race riots, affirmative action programs, racial quotas, and government-imposed busing—all of which have seriously divided blacks and whites. (Ted Kennedy has not been so fortunate in this respect.) Similarly, JFK's name commonly evokes memories of the soaring rhetoric of the inaugural address and the American triumph in the missile crisis, but not of the horrors of Vietnam and the arms race. In the popular perception, Kennedy is also seen as a president who served the interests of the poor and downtrodden, but he does not share blame for expensive entitlement programs. It may indeed be a special irony of Kennedy's image that it has profited from his inability to achieve some of the prime objectives of his presidency, for that failure has allowed Kennedy to escape responsibility for the problems that followed his death.

Early Critics

It is a tribute to the pervasive appeal of the Kennedy image in the 1960s that articulate dissent from it was confined largely to a small number of ideologues and intellectuals. (It should be added here, however, that the American political spectrum—especially on the Left—was considerably more truncated in the early 1960s than it would become later in the decade.) The right-wing critique of Kennedy is easily summarized. In screwball form, it embraced the thesis that Kennedy had been a willing agent of the worldwide Communist conspiracy and was killed because he failed to fulfill Moscow's designs quickly enough.[134] In its more respectable version, it argued that Kennedy had been a raw and naive leader who lacked sufficient toughness in his dealings with the Communists, held heretical views of economics, and erred in yielding to "extremists" in the civil rights movement.[135]

The left-wing critique of Kennedy was much more intellectually substantial and historically significant. Aspects of leftist criticism of Kennedy can be found in the writings of some of the late president's liberal admirers. William G. Carleton and Tom Wicker, to take just two examples, both suggested that Kennedy had failed to exert constructive leadership of the Congress. Carleton also added the observation that in his first two years in office, Kennedy "seems needlessly to have fanned the tensions of the dying Cold War."[136] But such criticism of Kennedy by liberals was largely of a concessive nature; it did not seriously mar their highly flattering portraits of JFK.

For more penetrating analyses of Kennedy's performance one must turn to the views of men somewhat to the left of Carleton and Wicker. Irving Howe, Milton Mayer, Hans Morgenthau, and Carey McWilliams all raised the problem of the great disparity between the grandiose promises projected by Kennedy's lofty rhetoric and the paucity of his concrete achievements. They also pointed to Kennedy's timid response to the civil rights movement, indicating that it was emblematic of his lack of moral conviction and commitment.[137] With characteristic iconoclasm, I. F. Stone suggested that Kennedy had been politically fortunate to die when he did, because he would not have to encounter the disenchantment that would attend the disappointment of the high hopes he had aroused in the country. Two articles by Stone that appeared in the *New York Review of Books* were prophetic of later "New Left" criticism of Kennedy's foreign policies. In one, he maintained that Kennedy's conduct in the missile crisis had been reckless, irresponsible, and politically motivated. In the other, he criticized the test ban as a public relations ploy that had shifted nuclear testing underground. Worse still, Stone wrote, Kennedy had agreed to the military's plea for accelerated arms tests in order to secure its support for the treaty.[138]

The most percipient early assessment of Kennedy's foreign policy was in an essay by George Kateb that appeared in *Commentary*. Kateb accepted Kennedy's claim to have injected a new "vigor" into American foreign policy. But for him, that was no cause for celebration. Instead, he deplored JFK's "break" with Eisenhower's policies for resulting in "the intensification of cold-war bellicosity, not in its lessening." The arms buildup and counterinsurgency were "much more" of a "provocation than a deterrent." Furthermore, because Kennedy chose to interpret every insurgency in the world as Soviet-supported or Soviet-inspired, "containment became a universal and undiscriminating principle of foreign policy." Hence Kennedy interpreted Laos and Vietnam as major-power confrontations and escalated American involvement in those two strategically unimportant countries. By the same token, his determination to maintain a balance between the two great power blocs had "led him to invest every direct Soviet-American problem with a high degree of passion." Because of his "intense desire to avoid giving the impression of weakness," Kennedy had escalated such problems into major tests of will. He had resumed nuclear testing after the Russians' resumption even though doing so served no useful purpose; likewise, he had issued a dramatic public ultimatum in the missile crisis, which unnecessarily backed Khrushchev into a corner.[139]

But even men of the Left were not immune to the appeal of aspects of the JFK image. Stone praised Kennedy for his reformist policies in Latin America, which he used to flail LBJ for his military intervention in the Dominican Republic.[140] Morgenthau endorsed the notion that Kennedy had begun to outgrow cold war dogmas in office.[141] Christopher Lasch, always a reliable barometer of shifts of the ideological climate on the Left, confessed in 1965 that he regretted not having voted in the 1960 presidential election. He, too, saw evidence of Kennedy's "growth" in the test ban treaty and the American University speech.[142] Even George Kateb, who was so scathingly critical of Kennedy for fueling cold war passions, speculated that the missile crisis caused him to reconsider his hard-line anti-Soviet stance. By Kateb's estimation, the test ban marked Kennedy's decision to reject the military's "passion for right appearances." Kateb also entertained the notion that Kennedy had won enough prestige from the arms treaty that he would have been able to prevail over his more "bellicose" aides had he lived longer.[143]

Revealingly, it was not Kennedy himself, but the glorified public image of him that most aroused the ire of social critics on both the Right and Left. Despite their ideological differences, critics of the Kennedy image converged on the view that the canonization of JFK and his family was symptomatic of the moral corruption and decadence of American society. What they disagreed about, of course, was the precise causes and nature of the malady. To Gore Vidal, "the cold-blooded jauntiness of the Kennedys in politics" appealed to those ruthlessly competitive Americans who found "the moral sense" both a burden and an annoyance. This was because the Kennedys' success made "hash" of "the old American belief that by working hard and being good one will deserve (and if fortunate, receive) promotion."[144] William F. Buckley, Jr., who crossed swords with Vidal at the 1968 Democratic convention, substantially agreed. To him, "the Kennedys' trinitarian (family, money, image) grasp on American life" had proved "enormously successful" because it engaged "the gears of a middle class that has pretty well abandoned its ideals, theological and moral."[145]

For Malcolm Muggeridge, the Kennedy story was a parable of the degradation of American politics by the allied forces of money and image making. Kennedy's "legend," he avowed, had been "systematically and deliberately created, paid for and propagated as part of an elaborately devised electioneering technique"; in the end, JFK wound up, like the contrived thing he was, "imprisoned in a legend."[146] Lasch's indictment was narrower in scope, but just as biting. He argued that the image of Kennedy as a glamorous yet "realistic" intellectual was the narcissistic fantasy of a generation of American intellectuals corrupted by the allure of power and worldly "success."[147] Midge Decter made a similar critique of the elitism of the Kennedy mystique. Unhampered by Lasch's left-democratic pieties, she extended her argument to cover the entirety of American society. In her view, the Kennedy administration had been "unquestionably successful" at imposing on the United States the image of itself "as the rightful, by virtue of intrinsic superiority, American ruling class." *Au fond*, the appeal of "Kennedyism" was "the assertion of the right to be ruled by attractive men, morally attractive, aesthetically attractive, in a morally, aesthetically attractive society." It was the myth of an aspiring "Establishment" that proposed to preside over "a great conservative imperial power."[148]

Significantly, the most far-reaching early critiques of Kennedy were penned by foreign observers of the American scene—Henry Fairlie and Henry Pachter. To both these men, reared in the denser ideological climate of Europe, the most salient aspect of the Kennedy legacy was its intellectual vacuity. As Pachter expressed it, "Kennedy was committed only to total commitment, but to no particular idea." Having "made a virtue out of his disdain for ideologies," Kennedy failed to understand movements for change and thus failed to build a popular coalition like FDR's; this, Pachter saw as one of the reasons for Kennedy's paucity of legislative successes.[149] Fairlie agreed. To him, Kennedy lacked "any whole view of the political community of the United States, of the point it had reached and the opportunities which awaited it." As a consequence, Kennedy "left concepts of political rights and obligations unaltered and unenriched"; "the 'New Frontier' was a limited exercise in civilizing the status quo." JFK's "vision of politics," Fairlie complained, "was almost entirely a vision of political method."[150]

Pachter's analysis of Kennedy's "pragmatism" formed the foundation of his attack on several major aspects of the Kennedy image. Pachter was quick to smell out the elitism underlying the portrait of Kennedy as a "pragmatist" who esteemed rational management over ideology. Because Kennedy "wanted to do everything *for* the people but nothing *through* the people," he had "nobody to lead and no cause to fight for." Consequently, he made *"himself"* the cause, basing the future on his own (and his wife's) charm, his wisdom and courage, and the "excellence" of his advisers. Here, then, was the genesis of Camelot. Kennedy's "elite of modernity" had "nothing" behind it, so it glorified Kennedy and his "myth," claiming to be fighting not American society, "but the Administration itself." This enabled it to blame the federal bureaucracy—especially the State Department—for all of Kennedy's failures, particularly in Vietnam. But to Pachter, all the New Frontiersmen's talk of "new ideas"— which they claimed could not be implemented because of bureaucratic resistance—merely disguised a poverty of intention. For example, the idea of "diversity" Kennedy enunciated in the American University speech was an empty one, because, unlike "democracy" or "socialism," it lacked substantive content. Furthermore, since it implicitly excluded the idea of a single, Communist world order, it was just a disguised form of cold war rhetoric.[151]

Pachter's essay ends with a vigorous reassertion of the ideal of intellectual independence, pointedly aimed at those "action intellectuals" who would make political power a standard of intellectual efficacy:

> The death of Kennedy . . . ended the reign of the Charles River team, the intellectual elite which had turned technocrats and managers. The myth is that it deprived America of the opportunity to be inspired by ideas. It is not the vocation of the idea-man to rule, it is his business to stand by, critically or encouragingly, but independently. He must not be identified with power, or else he loses contact with the sources of his ideas. Since men of power must always betray the ideas while they realize them, men of ideas must remain critics of power. This is how the mythmaker has betrayed the myth, and Schlesinger has forsaken Liberalism for Modernity.[152]

For all their brilliance, these observations of Pachter were of little immediate intellectual effect. They appeared in a little-known journal of opinion, and their assertion of the autonomy of the life of the mind would probably have been uncongenial to most American intellectuals in the 1960s, who made great claims for the "practical" role of ideas. Characteristically, when a wave of intellectually significant reassessments of Kennedy did appear, they were produced not by intellectuals content in their detachment from power, but by men and women intensely immersed in the controversies of their day.

3 ■ Kennedy Revised

The urge to reinterpretation is virtually universal. To revise one's view of the past from the perspective of the present is a common experience, as when the passionately held ideals of youth become puerile delusions in the cold, hard light of "mature" wisdom. As Peter Berger has written,

> common sense is quite wrong in thinking that the past is fixed, immutable, invariable, as against the ever-changing flux of the present. On the contrary, at least within our own consciousness, the past is malleable and flexible, constantly changing as our recollection reinterprets and re-explains what has happened. Thus we have as many lives as we have points of views [sic]. We keep reinterpreting our biography very much as the Stalinists kept rewriting the Soviet Encyclopedia, calling forth some events into decisive importance as others were banished to ignominious oblivion.[1]

A similar process occurs in the historical judgment of public figures. This is not only because the actions of politicians and statesmen are constantly reinterpreted from new viewpoints; it is also due to the necessarily ambiguous and complex effects of public conduct. As Shakespeare might have put it, both the good and bad done by a political leader lives after him, and the meaning of his legacy must be reevaluated constantly in view of the *consequences* of his acts, which may take years or decades to become clear.

It was inevitable, then, that John F. Kennedy would become the subject of historical revisionism. With equal predictability, the revisionists were sometimes accused of trying to rewrite history. But "history," in the commonly understood sense of a universally accepted and immutable view of the past, does not exist; there are only personal interpretations of events written by fallible human beings with their own biases and preconceptions. There was certainly never a single, indisputable view of Kennedy, even in the period of canonization immediately after the assassination. What is more, as I have shown above, the view of Kennedy promulgated by his admirers was itself subjected to revision when it came to such politically sensitive matters as the Vietnam War and JFK's relationship with Lyndon Johnson. In this sense, revisionism was begun by Kennedy's hagiographers, only to be continued by men and women with entirely different objectives in mind.

[I]

The revisionist critique of Kennedy and his record in office did not arise primarily from new facts or evidence, though the Pentagon Papers, which were released in 1971, helped clarify JFK's role in increasing American involvement in Vietnam.[2] Rather, revisionism had its origins in a new frame of reference. The prevailing positive image of Kennedy had grown out of the "pragmatic" liberalism of the early 1960s. Seen from such a vantage, Kennedy seemed a fresh and invigorating leader who had awakened the country from the supposed torpor and conservatism of the Eisenhower era. But revisionism reflected the disintegration of the cold war consensus on the containment of communism and disenchantment with the liberal legacy in domestic policy. Seen from this new perspective, Kennedy seemed to be a conventional cold warrior and an unimaginative and perhaps even conservative politician, who bore substantial responsibility for the woes of the Johnson-Nixon years: an escalating arms race, widening military entanglements abroad, racial turmoil, and abuses of presidential power.[3] The product of a wide-ranging reconsideration of the ideological limitations of American liberalism by radicals and even some liberals, much of the revisionist literature on Kennedy bore the intellectual imprint of the so-called "New Left."[4]

Seen from this new angle of vision, at some remove from the preconceptions of conventional American politics, Kennedy appeared anything but the bold innovator depicted by his admirers. The revisionists impatiently put aside all the talk of the profound impact of JFK's "style" and personality on American manners and policy; the obsessive concentration on Kennedy the man that one finds in his protagonists' writings is largely absent in the revisionist canon. William O'Neill echoed the dominant revisionist tone when he described the shift from Ike to JFK as one from "blandness" to "bombast," and complained that Kennedy made it seem that the cold war "would be won on the squash courts and dance floors of Washington." Similarly, Ronald Steel dismissed the vaunting rhetoric of the inaugural address as mostly "posturing heroics" and "tired cliches in vinyl wrappings."[5] Neither did the revisionists find much fresh substance in Kennedy's ideas and achievements. Despite his supposed freedom from "dogmas," "pieties," and "myths," Kennedy had acted in accordance with assumptions that exerted all the more power over him because of his lack of awareness of them. To Bruce Miroff, Kennedy had been "a prisoner of the most fundamental American myths and biases," most notably "the Cold War struggle against international communism, the regulated growth of a corporate economy, [and] the process of democratic reform through incremental legislation." For just this reason, he epitomized to Steel the failures of American liberalism, which had no "solutions for the ailments of modern society" other than the "formulas" of an "all-powerful bureaucracy, an unhindered President, and military intervention."[6]

According to the revisionists, Kennedy's captivity to the past—and thus his failures—was most evident in his management of foreign policy. Here, Kennedy and his advisers had behaved in accordance with a cold war consensus shared by both major parties. They had envisioned a world shaped by a balance of power between the Communist and non-Communist nations, believed that economic growth under capitalist auspices could spread democracy, tended to equate revolution in the Third World with the advance of communism, and had sought to preserve American client states as buffers against perceived Soviet expansionism.[7] What Kennedy added to this consensus, and often with disastrous consequences in the eyes of the revisionists, was a determination to prosecute the cold war with a new sophistication and "toughness." This change—a matter of style and technique more than substance—was ascribed to a variety of influences: Kennedy's military experience; the historical conditioning of his generation, which feared "appeasement" and believed that the "containment" of communism had been largely successful; a fear, especially common among Democrats accused of "losing" China, of appearing "soft on communism"; and JFK's family-induced concern with proving his masculinity.[8]

No matter what the sources to which they ascribed it, the revisionists universally deplored the "vigor" Kennedy injected into the American role in the cold war. Above all, the doctrine of "flexible response" and the attendant buildup of American arsenals were condemned for preventing the possibility of a major-power arms agreement, for causing the Soviets to engage in their own arms escalation, and for establishing the basis for expanded American intervention abroad, particularly in Vietnam. Worse still, "flexible response" had made the American response to foreign policy crises more rather than less rigid. The availability of more military options narrowed the alternatives actually perceived by policymakers by predisposing them to see crises as situations for which troops and armaments were a suitable response.[9]

But even Kennedy's admirers conceded the errors that stemmed from the "flexible response" doctrine. What, however, of JFK's supposed foreign policy initiatives toward the underdeveloped world—particularly his acceptance of a "world of diversity," his rejection of a dualistic view of every conflict in the Third World, and his refusal to impose American institutions abroad? When seen through the lens of revisionism, those allegedly bold innovations shrank to very modest proportions. To be sure, several revisionist writers praised Kennedy for his respectful dealings with Third World (particularly African) leaders and for his willingness to accept neutrality as an alternative to alignment with either of the major-power blocs.[10] But for the revisionists, those changes of style could not hide the essentially conventional *objectives* of Kennedy's overtures to the Third World. In fact, insofar as Kennedy had added a certain sophistication to the American drive to prevent "wars of liberation," he qualified, in the words of Richard J. Walton, as "the great counterrevolutionary of the postwar world."[11]

To the revisionists, counterinsurgency was the perfect reflection of the Kennedyite response to discontent in the Third World. Typifying JFK's preference for style over substance, it proposed to adopt the *methods* of guerrillas in the underdeveloped world without answering the fundamental problems that gave rise to guerrillas in the first place. It was also characteristic of the United States' "intellectual and nationalist arrogance," in that it attempted to impose American ideas of modernization and democratic change on other countries.[12] Such flaws, in fact, seemed to the revisionists to be typical of JFK's ostensibly "revolutionary" changes in American aid policy. The Alliance for Progress, for instance, arose out of the fear of Castroite revolutions spreading across Latin America, rather than from genuine concern for the welfare of the peoples south of the United States. Although "new" in the sense that it abandoned "the familiar policy of support for dictatorships, corrupt oligarchs, and military coups," it still funneled aid through the very elites that benefited from the status quo. Inevitably—and, some revisionists suggested, designedly—the reforms it helped institute were palliative rather than deep-seated. What is more, it languished after the humiliation of Castro and the Russians in the missile crisis dispelled American fears about the spread of communism throughout Central and South America.[13]

As the revisionists saw it, the Kennedy administration's opportunistic use of the Alliance for Progress was symbolic of its entire policy toward Latin America—indeed, toward the entire underdeveloped world. Kennedy's policy of backing the "democratic left" was to serve *American* interests above all—it was the "best hope," as Richard Barnet put it, "of bringing moderation to Latin America without violence and without stirring up hatred for the *yanqui*." Although trumpeted as seeking fundamental change by peaceful means, the administration's policy excluded violent change only when it was perceived as not suiting American interests—that is, when it was of a revolutionary character. Thus the Kennedy administration had done nothing to help prevent a right-wing coup to overthrow Juan Bosch in the Dominican Republic because of Bosch's supposed ties with Communists. Similarly, Kennedy assisted in the destabilization of the Jagan regime in British Guiana because of its alleged connections with the extreme Left.[14]

But for the revisionists, the ultimate—and most disastrous—expression of Kennedy's resolve to combat Third World revolution was his escalation of the American role in Vietnam. Steel dramatically summarized the gravamen of their indictment when he described Vietnam as a "liberal's war," "conceived, promoted, and directed by intellectuals, fascinated with power and eager to prove their toughness and resolve."[15] As Barnet put it, Kennedy saw Vietnam as a "test case" for counterinsurgency and applied there all the

new techniques at hand to head off an indigenous "war of liberation." For this reason, it best dramatized the fundamental errors of
Kennedy's counterrevolutionary strategies: the tendency to equate
revolution with communism, the arrogant faith in the United States'
ability to manipulate the internal politics of other countries, the
view of communism as a monolith, and the delusion that the *tactics*
of guerrillas could work, even when separated from their *objectives*.
The revisionists repudiated the claim of some of Kennedy's admirers
that their hero had come to see the error of his ways. Kennedy never
repudiated the doctrines underlying his expansion of the American
presence in Vietnam, and, as Steel pointed out, "despite his much-
quoted statement that it was South Vietnam's war to win, he never
gave any indication that he would allow Saigon to lose, and rejected
opportunities to withdraw."[16]

The revisionist case against Kennedy was based above all on the
inescapable fact of his escalation of the United States' part in the
conflict. Kennedy, the revisionists observed, had increased the
American presence in Southeast Asia above the level allowed by the
Geneva accords; he had sent the Green Berets to Vietnam; he had
initiated covert operations against North Vietnam; and he had authorized American "advisers" to provide combat support for the
South Vietnamese. Perhaps even more fatefully, he had deepened the
United States' psychological stake in Vietnam as a testing ground of
American resolve in the fight against communism. He had done this
by increasing American aid to Vietnam, with the intent of making it
a showplace of how economic development could head off Communist revolution. (The calamitous "strategic hamlet" program, which
attempted to isolate villagers from the sources of rebellion in newly
built settlements, was one egregious offspring of that policy.) Kennedy also meddled ineptly in the internal politics of the Diem regime, deepening American responsibility for the later course of
events in Vietnam. Most significant of all, JFK and his advisers raised
the symbolic stakes in Vietnam through rhetoric portraying it as a
major battleground between freedom and communism. For these
reasons, Barnet accused the Kennedy administration of having "set
in motion" the forces that made the United States' massive military
intervention in Southeast Asia "inevitable." Arguments about historical inevitability aside, the revisionists agreed that there was an
essential continuity between the Vietnam policies of the Kennedy
and Johnson administrations.[17]

From the revisionist perspective, the famous foreign policy crises of the Kennedy administration fell into a pattern quite unlike that plotted by JFK's adherents. Rather than demonstrating Kennedy's realism, flexibility, and growth, they actually manifested his hopeless unregeneracy as a cold warrior. In the revisionist view, the Bay of Pigs was not an aberration that served to teach Kennedy the follies of trusting "experts," the CIA, and his own luck, but was instead entirely consistent with JFK's crusading zeal to fight communism in the Third World and his inability to accept the legitimacy of left-wing revolutions in the underdeveloped world.[18] The Vienna conference was not a confrontation between a reasonable Kennedy and an inflexibly aggressive Khrushchev. Quite the contrary—all the Soviet premier sought was the legitimization of the status quo in Central Europe. (The revisionists tended to dismiss as bluster the Russian leader's threats to close off access to Berlin.) But Kennedy, fearful of appearing weak or irresolute in the wake of the Cuban fiasco, manipulated the Berlin issue to provide himself with an opportunity for making a show of "toughness." Reviving the already discredited alarmist rhetoric of his election campaign, he depicted Berlin as a major test of American will in order to justify a massive buildup of the United States' conventional and nuclear forces. In the process, he destroyed any opportunity for a genuine arms limitation agreement between the two superpowers.[19]

In the revisionists' view, the Soviets' decision to insert missiles in Cuba was an understandable (if not entirely defensible) response to the provocations of Kennedy's first year in office. Khrushchev, as they saw it, was seeking to make up for the growing Soviet disadvantage in the nuclear arms race caused by the Kennedy arms buildup. Moreover, the Cubans, shaken by the Bay of Pigs and JFK's missionary rhetoric about the struggle against communism around the globe, wanted the missiles to prevent any future invasion of their island nation. But, refusing to acknowledge his own part in bringing on the crisis, Kennedy simply interpreted it as another test of his will; several revisionists also suggested that he was concerned about the results of the 1962 elections if he appeared to be "soft on communism." Thus he never seriously considered the possibility of negotiations, despite the Soviet offer to remove the missiles in Cuba in exchange for the elimination of the admittedly "obsolete" American Jupiters in Turkey. Neither did the revisionists see much "restraint" in Kennedy's handling of the crisis. Instead of first resorting to diplomatic channels, JFK used television to announce the Soviet action and the American response, placing Khrushchev in the humiliating position where concessions on his part could only be interpreted as giving in to American ultimatums. That the crisis was finally resolved peacefully, then, was more a tribute to *his* reasonableness than to Kennedy's supposed flexibility and self-control.[20]

More disturbing still to the revisionists was the aftermath of the missile crisis. Seeing the withdrawal of the missiles as a victory of American "will" and "crisis management," Kennedy and his advisers were even more determined to show the Soviet Union that it could not prevail in national "wars of liberation," such as Vietnam.[21] Even the ban on all but underground testing of nuclear devices, so widely hailed as evidence of Kennedy's ripening wisdom to the dangers of nuclear catastrophe, was seen by revisionists as a portent of evil things to come. Led by I. F. Stone, they pointed out that the test ban treaty negotiations were preceded by Soviet offers of talks on a comprehensive agreement on limiting arms as well as tests, offers that were rejected by the Kennedy administration. Indeed, because of the United States' technological superiority at underground testing, the final agreement of 1963 was actually "sold" to the military and the public as the Soviets' acknowledgment of American nuclear superiority. Furthermore, in order to secure the Pentagon's approval of the treaty, Kennedy made concessions to the military, including an agreement to accelerate the underground testing of nuclear warheads. Since those tests eventually resulted in the development of the ABM and MIRV, the revisionists saw them as one of Kennedy's more fateful contributions to the arms race.[22]

[II]

Revisionism understandably focused on foreign policy, for it was there that Kennedy had exerted the greatest impact and that the failures of American policy were most obvious. But revisionists found serious evidence of the problems and limitations of "pragmatic" liberalism in other aspects of the Kennedy record and legacy. Instead of being the bold and pathbreaking program envisioned by his admirers, JFK's "New Economics" seemed to them to be a largely *conservative* device to rationalize and stabilize the American economy under corporate guidance. Although some of Kennedy's *personal* relations with businessmen were disharmonious (as shown by the U.S. Steel clash), and Wall Street had no fondness for JFK, his administration presented no danger to corporate power. Indeed, in his anxiety to placate business, Kennedy had decreased its tax burden early in his term. As his supposedly "revolutionary" tax bill moved through Congress, he agreed to modifications (including the elimination of significant tax reforms) that made it so regressive that it was acceptable to the U.S. Chamber of Commerce. Kennedy's conversion to Keynesianism, hence, was only to its more conservative implications—that is, tax cuts for business—while its more progressive aspects, such as increased spending on social welfare, were largely neglected during his term. Revisionists considered the central doctrines of Kennedy's Yale speech wholly consistent with the essentially conservative thrust of his economic policies. By stating, in effect, that future economic policy ought to be confined to "technical" management of problems by a technocratic elite, unhampered by ideological preconceptions, Kennedy implicitly debarred debate on the most fundamental economic issues—the power of the corporation and the system of class inequality from which it benefited.[23]

But to left-wing revisionists, nothing better symbolized the failures of Kennedyite liberalism than JFK's timid approach to the civil rights movement. For them, it represented a classic instance of the inadequacy of liberal leadership, with its preference for gradual, incremental change through established elites, when confronted with a democratic and moralistic movement that sought its objectives by direct, participatory means. As O'Neill saw it, Kennedy "was never much interested in civil rights or civil liberties" and always gave it a low priority before and during his presidency. Unable because of his ideological inadequacies and lack of moral passion to understand the emotions that lay behind black protest, he felt few qualms about sacrificing civil rights to the objectives of his administration in foreign policy and economics. The concessions he made to the cause through executive action were minor and cosmetic and largely placatory in aim. He failed to fulfill a campaign promise to sign immediately a modest bill to outlaw discrimination in some housing and used his brother's Justice Department as a political lightning rod to draw off criticism that might otherwise be directed at himself. All the while, his administration moved slowly against discrimination and segregation and did little to protect civil rights workers against intimidation and assassination. Worse still, by emphasizing voting rights as an issue, it attempted to divert the civil rights movement into the most innocuous of channels.[24]

To the revisionists, Kennedy's eventual endorsement of major civil rights legislation did not represent any fundamental "growth" in the man. It reflected, rather, Kennedy's fear of losing control of the situation as both popular demonstrations and racial violence escalated. And the revisionists saw it as typical of Kennedy that he did not see how his earlier inaction on black grievances had contributed to the worsening of tension between the races. In domestic as in foreign policy, Kennedy was more attuned to the management of "crises" (which were often of his own creation) rather than tackling basic, underlying problems. This failing was also evident, according to the revisionists, in Kennedy's lack of moral leadership on the question of civil rights. Because he chose gradual, incremental, and piecemeal approaches to the racial crisis, Kennedy failed to educate Americans of both races in how biracial harmony and justice could be achieved. In this respect, he was faulted for having contributed to the racial polarizations of the late 1960s.[25]

Some revisionist criticism of Kennedy extended beyond his major initiatives in foreign and domestic policy. One writer condemned the Peace Corps as a public relations device to give American imperialism a patina of reformist respectability by exploiting the talents and idealism of well-meaning volunteers.[26] Several revisionists attacked the space program as another instance of Kennedy's badly misplaced sense of priorities. To them, the one-sided "race to the moon" was a bathetic and wasteful tribute to Kennedy's obsession with besting the Russians and with symbols of national prestige.[27] Finally, the cult of strong, personalized presidential leadership celebrated by Kennedy's liberal admirers was attacked for opening the way to some of the worst excesses of Johnson and Nixon. Some revisionists saw a direct connection between Kennedy's "charismatic," personality-based leadership style and his successors' abuses in Vietnam and the Watergate scandal.[28] Others were content to suggest that Kennedy's tendency to invest his office with some of the attributes of royalty had created powerful temptations to corruption and the indulgence of egomania. In either case, Kennedy, and such intellectual glorifiers of executive power as Arthur M. Schlesinger, Jr., was seen as sharing culpability for the evils of overreaching presidential power. Having seen how presidential authority could be used for ends of which they did not approve, even liberals recoiled from the notion that an activist, powerful presidency was needed to overcome the forces of inertia in the federal bureaucracy and of conservatism in Congress. Professor Edwin Hargrove of Brown University posed the liberals' dilemma baldly: "Did we liberals idealize power too much?" His answer was characteristic of the repentant revisionist: "We did—we had a progressive theory of American history that virtue centered in the executive."[29]

[III]

Although often grouped with revisionist works on Kennedy, David Halberstam's *The Best and the Brightest* bears but a loose filial resemblance to them. Like the revisionists, Halberstam portrayed the escalation of the American role in Vietnam as the result of preoccupations that gained ascendancy under JFK—the concern to imbue foreign policy with "toughness," the delusory high hopes underlying counterinsurgency, and the hubris of rational management. But to Halberstam, these qualities were best typified *not* by Kennedy but by the experts and technocrats mocked in the title of his book. Those men—usually Ivy League–educated and often schooled in the Office of Strategic Services during World War II—Halberstam saw as a self-conscious elite who sought to infuse the United States with their own sense of imperial mission. But to Halberstam, JFK always maintained a detached and skeptical perspective on the advice of these national security managers. Indeed, his narrative suggests—although speculatively—that Kennedy gradually, though incompletely, disengaged himself from their assumptions and beliefs, at least insofar as they applied to Vietnam.[30]

Halberstam's argument, then, implicitly endorsed the thesis of "growth." According to Halberstam, Kennedy "probably" became skeptical of expert advice after the Bay of Pigs disaster, and the missile crisis made him wary of "the institutional wisdom of force in many areas of the world." This skepticism, along with the Buddhist revolt against Diem, made him increasingly receptive to pessimistic estimates of the American position in Vietnam. Halberstam wisely refused to speculate about what Kennedy might have done had he lived longer, and he did criticize JFK for deepening the American role in Vietnam and concealing its extent from the public. But the unmistakable impression left by his book is that Kennedy was awakening to the realization that the American involvement in Vietnam was a mistake and that he was at least prepared to consider withdrawal. *The Best and the Brightest* is largely undocumented, however, making it difficult to assess the sources of its statements about

Kennedy's ideas and emotions. And many of Halberstam's descriptions of Kennedy's thoughts and moods are admittedly speculative, allowing one to entertain the suspicion that his thesis is an a priori projection of his own wishful thinking. Halberstam is an admirer of the Kennedys—especially Robert Kennedy—and it requires no difficulty to see in his book a tendency to place the thoughts of RFK in 1968 in the mind of JFK in 1963.[31]

[IV]

The revisionist view of Kennedy did not arise only from a new ideological perspective. It also reflected the emergence of a new sensibility, manifested by such diverse phenomena as the so-called "counterculture," the resurgence of feminism, the environmental movement, and more favorable public attitudes toward homosexuality. Although the precise nature and origins of this new sensibility have yet to be satisfactorily explored, it can be said to have involved a questioning of long-held assumptions about the relations of the sexes and the roles of emotion and rationality in human life. Inevitably, Kennedy came within the critical scrutiny of the advocates of the new cultural *Weltanschauung*. In a fascinating transvaluation of values, Kennedy's cult of masculine efficacy was reinterpreted as *macho* posturing, his emphasis on competitive achievement was denounced as capitalist and imperialist, and his pursuit of rational management was seen as reaching its ultimate expression in the cold-blooded "bureaucratic homicide" visited upon the peasants of Vietnam. But in most revisionist works on Kennedy, such characterizations were little more than casual asides, not pursued in any depth or detail.[32] Only in Nancy Gager Clinch's *The Kennedy Neurosis* was there a large-scale attempt to probe the cultural underpinnings of JFK's behavior and policies.[33]

By any standard, the Kennedys are inviting subjects for the psychoanalyst. But Clinch's book is not really a work of psychoanalysis; it is rather an ideological polemic done up in the fashionable academic garb of psychohistory. Clinch rejected Freudian depth psychology, for its emphasis on *internal* psychic conflicts and the sense of the moral complexity of social life were incompatible with her objective of deriving simple moral lessons from the Kennedy saga. She relied instead on ego psychology, which, because it stresses the individual's *conscious* adjustments to the external environment, allowed her to assign to the Kennedys personal responsibility (blame?) for their actions. Furthermore, she relied on a specific form of ego psychology—the "humanistic psychology" of Erich Fromm, Abraham Maslow, and Rollo May. The reason for this is obvious. "Psychohumanism" has a normative model of human behavior—as "constantly striving toward loving relationships, social cooperation, and self-actualization"—that permitted Clinch to smuggle into her psychological framework the intellectual perspectives of feminism and the New Left. Thus, in Clinch's analysis, the categories of psychoanalysis are employed for tendentious purposes; deviation from a proper, ideologically "healthy" mode of behavior is equated with sickness.[34]

With the intellectual apparatus of *The Kennedy Neurosis* on full display, its argument and conclusions are easily understood. The "Kennedy neurosis" is "a drive to power and dominance of others rather than a drive for equality, love and sharing." Inculcated in the Kennedy children by their excessively competitive and conformist parents, who sought to fulfill through their offspring their own unsatisfied needs for acceptance and preeminence in American society, it revealed itself most obviously in the Kennedy sons' ruthless drive for success and dominance, indifference to others, and manipulative treatment of women. Less obviously, it manifested itself in suppressed rage toward the Kennedy parents, which showed itself in the Kennedy sons' self-destructive behavior and JFK's numerous physical ailments. Clinch also found evidence of the Kennedy neurosis in JFK's cool response to the civil rights movement, compulsive need for competitive victories in foreign policy, and obsession with such symbols of prestige as the race to the moon.[35]

The Kennedy Neurosis is easily criticized. It is repetitive, argumentative, and extremely speculative, as shown by Clinch's frequent use of the conditional tense when evidence failed her.[36] A more disturbing aspect of the book, and an ironic one in light of the professed "humanism" of its author, is its tendency to dehumanize its subjects. This is because Clinch's real objective was not to criticize the Kennedys themselves but to use them as symbolic targets of her ideological critique of western culture. At one point, she attacked the Kennedy mystique as "essentially the outcome of some four thousand years of the Graeco-Judeo-Christian ethos," embodying "the conquest of nature and death through obsessive activism and human competition"—surely some of the most sophomoric prose ever written. Of course, by stating her thesis in such grandiose terms, Clinch undermined it; for if the Kennedys merely personify the faults of the Occident, their neurosis is one in which we all share to some degree and for which they are no more deserving of condemnation than the rest of us. One might easily turn Clinch's argument about and charge *her* with a form of neurosis—what might be called the "left-wing neurosis" (the temptation to call it the "Clinch neurosis" will be resisted). Simply stated, this malady consists of judging men and women by abstract and unrealistic standards of moral perfection. Insofar as it reflects this affliction, *The Kennedy Neurosis* is typical of much left-wing revisionism, in which concepts of "humanity" and "love" served to sanction an intense malice toward flesh-and-blood human beings.[37]

While *The Kennedy Neurosis* criticizes Kennedy for falling short of idealized goals, Henry Fairlie's *The Kennedy Promise* attacks him for having promised too much.[38] This is an idiosyncratic book, written by a man who was an odd fish in the American political setting. Fairlie was an English admirer of the High Tory conservatism of Professor Michael Oakeshott, whose main intellectual project has been to narrowly delimit the sphere of the "political." His chief quarrel with the modern state is precisely that it has overstepped its boundaries.[39] Similarly, Fairlie's primary complaint with Kennedy was that he unduly raised Americans' expectations of their political leaders through his cult of personalized presidential leadership. In Oakeshottian fashion, Fairlie found fault with Kennedy's "politics of expectation" because it tried to endow the American people with a sense of collective purpose—an objective that, as a good Tory, Fairlie considered properly within the sphere of religion. This central argument was yoked, somewhat awkwardly, to a New Left interpretation of Kennedy's foreign and domestic policies. Like the left revisionists, Fairlie attacked Kennedy for inflating the public's perception of the United States' role in the world through millennial cold war rhetoric. But unlike most of the revisionists, Fairlie had in mind no positive alternative to Kennedy's policies; his critique of New Frontier rhetoric was not merely that it overstated the capabilities of American power but that it encouraged the people to "expect too much of their political institutions and their political leaders." The strongest part of Fairlie's argument was his discussion of Kennedy's penchant for "guerrilla government"—the reliance on personal leadership to bypass regular institutional channels. Fairlie found this phenomenon manifested in diverse ways—counterinsurgency, "crisis management," the "politics of theater," and Kennedy's reliance on his personal and familial retinue rather than on the federal bureaucracy to get things done. All these things, Fairlie claimed, encouraged the people to believe that JFK "would intrude on their behalf, if not with a divinity, at least with the forces which governed their lives."[40]

One need not accept the Oakeshottian framework of Fairlie's argument to allow that he pointed to an important aspect of the Kennedy presidency. So far as matters of *tone* are concerned, Fairlie would seem to have been correct when he claimed that the New Frontier held out the grandiose promise of *transcending* politics. Appropriately enough, Fairlie traced some of the origins of Kennedy's mystique of personal leadership to English influences, particularly to the aristocratic ideals projected in the writings of one of Kennedy's favorite authors, John Buchan.[41] But for all the grace, wit, and penetration with which it is presented, Fairlie's thesis was badly overargued. The central, unexamined premise of *The Kennedy Promise* is that Kennedy was absolutely determinative of the tenor and tone of American politics during his presidency. This assumption led Fairlie into a portentousness of overstatement that would have embarrassed even Schlesinger. Is it really true, one feels tempted to ask, that Kennedy kept the United States in "an atmosphere of perpetual crisis and of recurring crisis" throughout his administration? One may ask, too, if rhetoric has the compulsive power Fairlie seemed to ascribe to it. If the American people did respond to Kennedy's oratory, might it have been because circumstances, and not just Kennedy's brilliance as a speaker, made them receptive to it? At least with respect to one major issue, civil rights, the vast majority of Americans remained remarkably unmoved by Kennedy's lofty words.[42]

What is more—and somewhat incongruous in a book by a self-identified conservative—Fairlie never considered the importance of *institutions* in shaping Kennedy's style of leadership. It may have been possible, for instance, that Kennedy's reliance on the mass media of communication simply reflected a realistic assessment of how a modern politician can reach and influence the mass public. Furthermore, Fairlie did not devote much attention to how institutions may have *limited* Kennedy's freedom of action. He argued that Kennedy's failures as a leader were inherent in the "politics of expectation," which by unreasonably inflating hopes must inevitably disappoint them. But he ignored such mundane considerations as the conservative majority in Congress and the preponderance of southern congressional committee chairmen.[43] Such problems, of course, would have raised questions about the importance of "the politics of expectation," something Fairlie was understandably inclined not to do. But the result of this failing was ironic, for in making Kennedy's mode of leadership so central to his interpretation, Fairlie implicitly accepted the New Frontiersmen's claim that Kennedy had radically altered the style of American politics.[44]

[V]

Although revisionism bulked large in the debate over JFK's life and legacy in the late 1960s and early 1970s, its influence does not seem to have extended far beyond certain liberal and academic circles. Some of the disillusionments it expressed were easily vulgarized into the trendy clichés retailed in Robert Patrick's play, *Kennedy's Children*.[45] But the alienation from national ideas and ideals it expressed did not penetrate very deeply into American society, as evidenced by the disastrous defeat of the presidential candidate of the "new politics" (ironically, a Kennedy follower) in 1972. A Harris poll in 1973 indicated that Kennedy remained, by an overwhelming margin, the most popular of American presidents.[46] Even on the Left, revisionism did not sweep all before it. In a poll of historians (most of whom tend to be liberal), Kennedy received high grades for idealism and flexibility.[47] The conception of Kennedy as an incipient social democrat also displayed remarkable persistence. Two popular novels on the assassination that were made into films, *Executive Action*[48] and *Winter Kills*,[49] depicted Kennedy as the victim of reactionary oligarchs distressed by the ostensible leftward drift of his administration. It was true as well that the watery values of the new sensibility could be assimilated easily to New Frontier idealism and youth worship. This was most appallingly shown by the *schwarmerei* of Leonard Bernstein's *Mass*, composed for the official opening of the John F. Kennedy Center for the Performing Arts in 1971.[50]

Kennedy revisionism also—and inevitably—prompted Kennedy counterrevisionism. Much of the defense of JFK rested, as always, on his supposed contribution of intangibles to American life. Richard Boeth praised Kennedy for having "made people feel good about themselves, and confident of their ability to take responsibility for their own lives." Anthony Lewis extolled JFK for instilling his countrymen with "hope," "confidence," and "trust," and for his "sense of nobility," "ability to admit error," and openness to criticism and new ideas. Andrew Greeley wrote that Kennedy's "decisive contribution" to the country was that he "made politics interesting again." The tenth anniversary of the Kennedy assassination fell in the midst of the Watergate scandal, providing JFK's admirers with a dramatic backdrop against which they could contrast their hero's virtues with Nixon's duplicity and stealth. Schlesinger thus exalted Kennedy for enabling Americans to "respect and trust their government," and Sorensen noted wistfully that politics had been a "noble profession" when JFK sat in the White House. On more substantive grounds, the revisionists were criticized for excessive stridency and a lack of historical proportion. This charge had some point, as when Tom Wicker complained that left-wing journalists and historians placed at Kennedy's door "virtually the entire history of the subsequent decade." Suzannah Lessard detected the element of generational revolt in the writings of the younger revisionists and wrote that "our dismissal of Kennedy came too easily, ricocheting off the shock of our parents and our amazed and immature perception of events."[51]

Some writers also suggested that the revisionists were guilty of not considering the historical context within which Kennedy operated. In their opinion, the revisionist perspective was distorted because it did not take into account that most of the pressures on Kennedy were from the *Right*, not the *Left*. Judged in the light of the prevailing cold war atmosphere of his time, Kennedy indeed appeared more judicious and less aggressive than revisionism implied. Abram Chayes, for instance, observed that in the missile crisis, Kennedy had rejected an air strike against Cuba, allowed two Russian ships to return home unmolested, and had deferred retaliation for the shooting down of two American spy planes. "This is not the picture," Chayes declared scoldingly, "of a man engaged in a test of wills to be pursued to the end, but of one anxious to avoid an armed engagement at any acceptable cost. Indeed, there were many in the government who, upon hearing of these decisions, believed the President had caved in."[52] Robert M. Slusser made much the same observation about Kennedy's role in the Berlin crisis. He pointed to the many pressures on Kennedy to take a harder line toward the Russians, which he contrasted with the president's "essentially reactive" response to the construction of the Berlin Wall and his continued search for negotiations after its completion.[53]

The most substantial attempt to defend Kennedy from the charge that he had unduly concentrated presidential power came in Schlesinger's *The Imperial Presidency*. This is an odd—some would say hypocritical—book, coming from the man who did most to glorify the activist presidency as a progressive force in American history. Much of its argument is defensive, trying to exculpate Kennedy from the excesses of Johnson and Nixon. Part of Schlesinger's strategy was simply to share the blame; he claimed that both liberals and conservatives shared in the "presidential mystique" of the 1960s. But most of Schlesinger's argument repeated the familiar stock formulae. Part of his argument referred to "growth"; Schlesinger asserted that the Bay of Pigs provided Kennedy with "a salutary if costly lesson in the perils of presidential isolation," which led to his widespread consultations during the missile crisis. Another part referred to matters of "style" and character; Schlesinger claimed that Kennedy's "ironic and skeptical intelligence customarily kept the presidency in healthy perspective." When all else failed, Schlesinger resorted to the familiar excuse that Kennedy's choices were limited by institutions and circumstances. He thus wrote that Kennedy had "no alternative" to unilateral executive action in the missile crisis because of the need to maintain secrecy. Furthermore, he declared, congressional consultations would not have changed Kennedy's policies anyway because most congressmen would have agreed with them.[54]

[VI]

Arising as it did from a perspective "outside" the boundaries of conventional American politics, the revisionist literature on Kennedy brought a new and largely beneficial sense of proportion to the image of JFK's role in history. By revealing the previously unquestioned premises underlying Kennedy's actions, it helped scale down dramatically the extravagant claims made for his boldness and originality. Indeed, the theme of Kennedy's uncritical acceptance of established ideas and assumptions, stripped of the revisionists' opprobrious judgments, would later be incorporated into more "balanced" accounts of his presidency.[55] But the revisionists' insights into JFK's essential conventionality were purchased at some price. For one thing, the assessments they made of Kennedy and his policies often took inadequate account of historical context. Without accepting the argument that certain prevalent ideas (such as the beliefs underlying the cold war) or institutions (such as the military) *compelled* Kennedy to act in certain ways, one must allow that they did establish boundaries within which he could function effectively. What is more, any judgment of a democratic leader's innovativeness or moral courage (two qualities the revisionists found sadly deficient in Kennedy) must make allowance for those limits. Thus, while the revisionists' finding that Kennedy was, in many respects, a conventional politician may help dispel the inflated claims about his "revolutionary" impact, it tells us little about his accomplishments when judged by the standards of his time. To be sure, some of the revisionists betrayed an awareness of this matter when they described Kennedy as the "captive" or "prisoner" of certain inarticulate attitudes and preconceptions. But the revisionists' censorious tone toward Kennedy, along with their implied prescriptions of what he *should* have done about certain problems, would easily lead one to the conclusion that Kennedy's limitations were purely personal, rather than reflections of the inadequacies of the American social and political systems.

The revisionists were also guilty on occasion of intellectual arrogance and anachronism. A noteworthy instance of this is O'Neill's account of JFK's civil rights policies. Like other left-wing critics of Kennedy, O'Neill criticized the president for being unduly cautious and opportunistic in his dealings with the black movement for racial equality. However, he also had to concede that Kennedy's policies seem to have been overwhelmingly popular with the black rank-and-file. Confronted by this seeming paradox, O'Neill argued that "the pleasure they derived from seeing white racist power humbled in Mississippi helped reconcile many Negroes to the slow pace of integration [and] to the administration's failure to protect civil rights workers in the South from intimidation as well as assassination. Here, as elsewhere, public relations bridged the gap between promise and performance."[56] This is tortuous (if not tortured) reasoning; and though one may legitimately ask whether Kennedy did enough to justify such wide support among blacks, one somehow suspects that they were better judges of the situation than O'Neill, writing with all the benefit of historical retrospect.

Finally, the revisionists seem to have had little sense of the ironies and contradictions of the historical process. In their eagerness to demolish Kennedy's reputation as a bold and "progressive" leader, they tended, like his admirers, to overstate his role in events. They paid too little heed to how forces beyond JFK's control often made his policies lead to results he did not desire and certainly could not have foreseen. An obvious example of this was the doctrine of "flexible response." Kennedy seems to have sincerely believed that this doctrine, when put into effect, would help prevent wars and superpower confrontations. That in fact it had the opposite effect—an important point made by the revisionists—may be a reflection of how good intentions may be distorted by what Hegel called "the cunning of reason." But in any historical assessment of the doctrine, those good intentions (and not just the baleful results) should figure in the reckoning.[57]

With the revisionist attack on the prevailing positive orthodoxy, interpretations of Kennedy seemed to have completed a cycle of stimulus and response. The spokesmen of a transitory mood in intellectual circles, the revisionists had their heyday of creativity and influence in the late 1960s and early 1970s, though articles and books in a revisionist mold continue to be written, and revisionist influences live on in textbooks, which have often served as repositories of moribund historical fashions.[58] But surprisingly, a new wave of reconsiderations of Kennedy was in the offing in the mid-1970s, prompted by revelations from unexpected sources.

4 ■ Kennedy Revealed

If contemporary American politics has any distinctive and salient quality, it is the erosion of the barriers between the private and public realms. Largely as a result of the media of mass communication, the process of voting has become more and more analogous to the consumer's "choice" of commodities. Increasingly, to cast a vote for a candidate is seen as an act of self-definition in which one selects an "image" supposedly emblematic of one's "taste" and "lifestyle." If the Kennedys have any claim to being the pioneers of the "new politics," it is primarily because they were the first to sense fully the political uses of "style." It is *they* who have used the picture magazines and television to project themselves as the ideal American family and who have tried to make good looks and glamour into major political assets. JFK's candidacies for the Democratic presidential nomination and the presidency were largely successful because of his masterful use of television to convey an appealing personality, and Kennedy himself declared of his administration, "We couldn't survive without TV."[1] But all this has had its price. The public's ever-growing awareness of how images can be manipulated has made it intensely curious about the realities behind the appealing facades presented by the Kennedys.[2] The Kennedys must therefore live in a glare of publicity and are constant subjects of gossip in the tabloids and scandal sheets. While they seek to endow their private lives with public virtues, so people seek to find public meaning in their personal affairs. Thus Chappaquiddick was perceived by many Americans not only as a question of justice but also as one of image; they were dismayed not only by what Edward Kennedy had done but also by his and his advisers' failure at the management of appearances.[3]

It was almost inevitable, then, that the reassessment of Kennedy would embrace his private life. Here, as with revisionism, the surprising thing was not the reassessment itself but the delay in its appearance. Rumors of sexual misconduct by Kennedy had been rife in Washington during his lifetime and were a common topic of gossip in the sensationalistic press after his death.[4] But the same sort of inhibitions that held back the reconsideration of Kennedy's public conduct seem to have prevented a similar review of his private life by the reputable press and news media. The desanctification of the Kennedy family, along with the public cynicism made fashionable by the Watergate scandal, helped lower some of those restraints. This first became evident in 1974, with the appearance of books by Norman Mailer and Earl Wilson that suggested possible sexual liaisons between Marilyn Monroe and one of the Kennedy brothers. Wilson lent credence to stories of a lengthy affair between JFK and Monroe, while Mailer toyed with but dismissed the possibility of an amorous involvement between Robert Kennedy and the suicidal actress. Neither's account said much that was original, and Wilson's was based heavily on gossip and rumor.[5] But the mere fact of the appearance of such speculation about the Kennedys' sexual lives indicated that a new territory of Kennedy reassessments was opening.

Suspicions about Kennedy's private life and character were further fueled by Ben Bradlee's *Conversations with Kennedy*. This is a curious book, both because of its author and contents. The Washington bureau chief of *Newsweek* during the Kennedy presidency, Bradlee had been a close personal friend of JFK and had written one of the most intensely personal tributes to Kennedy after the assassination.[6] He had also recently gained great notoriety and cachet as executive editor of the *Washington Post* during the Watergate scandal. *Conversations with Kennedy* is professedly his fond personal memoir of the Kennedy years, no doubt issued to provide a dramatic contrast to the seaminess of the Nixon years. But the book contains revelations that undermine its apparent intent; one critic perceptively noted its "emotional dyslexia." It has the usual lyrical clichés

about Kennedy's inspirational virtues—at one point, Bradlee wrote
that Kennedy "lit the skies of this land bright with hope and promise"—but much of what it reveals about Kennedy is less than flattering.[7]

Indeed, the picture of Kennedy that emerges from *Conversations
with Kennedy* bears disturbing similarities to the caricature by
Nancy Gager Clinch. The book shows Kennedy to have been coldly
manipulative and obsessively image-conscious; he used Bradlee to
promote his own political fortunes (though it should be added that
Bradlee did not object to being so used) but withdrew special personal
access when some mildly critical remarks by Bradlee were quoted in
Look. Kennedy eventually brought Bradlee back into his good graces,
but only when he could use him to counteract a potentially damaging story that he had concealed a former marriage.[8] And Kennedy
appears in the book as a conventional chauvinistic male, who coupled images of sex and domination. On many occasions, he compared
setbacks to being sodomized—the U.S. Steel price increase, to take
just one example, was a "cold, deliberate fucking"—and Bradlee
noted that he enjoyed James Bond films for "the cool and the sex and
the brutality."[9] Kennedy also appears as unfeeling and lacking in
empathy for others. At one point, Bradlee quoted him as saying that
he was all for people solving their problems by abortion. (One won-
ders what Cardinal Cushing would have thought of this!) Kennedy
also appears, most disturbingly, as quite cynical and perhaps even
corrupt. There is the suggestion that he may have known of chica-
nery by Mayor Daley and his "friends" to help secure his election,
and there is the admission that he put his personal valet and Jacqueline's maid on the public payroll. Bradlee also revealed that Kennedy had access to the income tax returns of J. Paul Getty and H. L.
Hunt—a particularly embarrassing revelation in light of the Ken-
nedyites' sanctimonious criticism of Nixon for his personal use of
private tax information. In the face of all this evidence (and more of a
similar nature), Bradlee invoked a "dichotomy" in the Kennedy character—"half the 'mick' politician, tough, earthy, bawdy, sentimental, and half the bright, graceful, intellectual *Playboy of the Western
World*." But the second half of this "dichotomy" is far less in evidence than the first in *Conversations with Kennedy*, which shows
JFK to have been in many ways a quite commonplace—and in some
respects very unpleasant—human being.[10]

The first substantive revelation of Kennedy's sexual infidelities came, appropriately enough, as the result of the national self-scrutiny after Watergate. In the course of an investigation into plots to murder foreign leaders, the Senate Select Committee on Intelligence, headed by Frank Church of Idaho, discovered personal connections between Kennedy and Judith Campbell. It also found that Campbell was an associate of two gangsters, John Roselli and Sam Giancana, who had participated in CIA plots to kill Castro. Suspecting that Campbell (who had recently married golfer Dan Exner) might have been a go-between for the president and the two gangsters, the Church committee subpoened her to testify secretly in September 1975. Her testimony, which indicated she had not known of the assassination plots, was kept secret and sealed for fifty years, and the committee decided that Exner should be referred to only as Kennedy's "friend" in its report.[11]

The committee's actions were consistent with the implicit code of mutual protection among politicians, not to refer to each other's private lives. They were also consistent with the ambitions of Senator Church, who was planning to seek the Democratic presidential nomination in 1976 and naturally did not want to alienate the Kennedys. But in the post–Watergate era, unpleasant truths were not easily swept under the rug. Four days before the official release of the Church committee's report, news of Exner's identity was leaked to the press. Appropriately enough, it was Bradlee's *Washington Post*, the *primum mobile* of investigative journalism, that broke the news on November 16, 1975. However, it relegated the story to its inside pages, confirming conservative suspicions of a journalistic double standard by the liberal paper.[12] Despite the *Post*'s gingerly treatment of the Campbell episode, right-wing journalists, led by William Safire, pounced on it. Their motives in doing so were transparent—they wanted to raise the stature of their hero Nixon by lowering that of one of his publicly revered predecessors.[13] Nevertheless, Safire raised some disquieting questions about the Church committee and the Campbell-Kennedy relationship that have never been answered satisfactorily. He pointed to the Kennedy family connections of several of the Church committee lawyers who had questioned Exner and suggested that there may have been a cover-up of a possible Kennedy-Mafia link. Safire also criticized the Church committee for failing to question Frank Sinatra about his role in introducing Campbell to both Kennedy and Giancana and about any knowledge he might have had of any CIA-Mafia plots.[14] In a separate investigative series for the

New York Times, Nicholas Gage revealed disturbing evidence that the Kennedy Justice Department may have gone easy on Roselli, perhaps to protect JFK from damaging revelations.[15]

Mrs. Exner's own description of her relationship with Kennedy stoked the fires of controversy. In a news conference on December 17, 1975, she confirmed that she had indeed been close to Kennedy during his presidency but refused to say whether she had been sexually intimate with him. Exner denied that she had possessed any knowledge of the assassination plots or that she had served as a conduit between the president and the mobsters. Her motives in calling the news conference, however, were suspect. Exner apparently wanted to reassure the Mafia that she had made no damaging revelations to the Church committee, and she also wanted to promote her own memoirs, which her agent would soon be peddling to publishers.[16] Exner's autobiography, which appeared in 1977, reiterated her story substantially but included confidential telephone numbers and addresses that made her claims more believable. Exner confirmed that she had in fact had an affair with Kennedy and added more material for the gossip columns and rumor mills. She implied that JFK had received injections (possibly of amphetamines) from Dr. Max Jacobson, the notorious "Dr. Feelgood"; claimed that JFK had said that his marriage was an unhappy one, from which Jacqueline had wanted out; and wrote that JFK had mused during one of their trysts over the prospect of establishing a family presidential dynasty, with himself as its patriarch.[17]

The Exner story seems to have blown the lid off the conspiracy of silence that had long hidden JFK's private life from public scrutiny. A succession of kiss-and-tell revelations poured from the presses in the mid-1970s, prompting one of Kennedy's admirers to ask how, if all the stories were true, JFK had ever had time to attend to his official duties.[18] Some of the most enduring stories were in the memoirs of a former White House kennel keeper, who recalled seeing naked women running about the family quarters of the Executive Mansion and sharing the pool with Kennedy and several of his cronies.[19] Most such accounts of Kennedy's affairs provided titillation and amusement, but one had disturbing implications. In February 1976 the *National Enquirer* published a story based on interviews with James Truitt, a former editor and executive assistant at the *Washington Post*. Truitt claimed that he had notes based on conversations he had with Mary Pinchot Meyer during the Kennedy presidency. According to Truitt, Meyer, the sister of Ben Bradlee's ex-wife Tony and the former wife of CIA official Cord Meyer, had told him of an affair she was having with Kennedy. Among other spicy revelations, Truitt's story alleged that Meyer had once said that Kennedy had offered to obtain cocaine for her while they were smoking marijuana. The Kennedy-Meyer affair took on darker undertones because Meyer had been murdered in October 1964 (her accused murderer had been acquitted), and her diary, which reportedly contained references to her involvement with JFK, was destroyed by a CIA agent.[20]

The revelatory literature on Kennedy reached a peak of iconoclastic relentlessness in Joan and Clay Blair, Jr.'s *The Search for JFK*. Based largely on confidential interviews with close friends of Kennedy, this book features further accounts of JFK's romantic and sexual affairs, including his entanglement during World War II with Inga Arvad, a Swedish photographer who may have had ties to the Nazis. It also purported to show that the PT-109 affair was the result of Kennedy's recklessness, and that JFK deserved little credit for the rescue of his crew. In addition, it adduced more supporting evidence for the persisting allegation that Kennedy had been afflicted with Addison's disease.[21]

The wave of revelations about Kennedy did not just raise questions about his private behavior and character. They also created doubts as to whether he was guilty of imposing his personal feelings on public policy. Such doubts were generated by the findings of the Church committee's investigation of the Castro assassination plots. With regard to its original objective—discovering whether Kennedy authorized or knew of the plots to kill the Cuban dictator—the committee arrived at no conclusive result. It simply could not find any definitive evidence that Kennedy was involved (or not involved) in the CIA's comic opera schemes to slip Castro an exploding cigar and poison his scuba suit. But the committee's other major discovery about Kennedy was in some respects more damaging than the revelation of direct involvement in the Castro murder plots might have been. It found that after the Bay of Pigs, Kennedy had authorized "Operation Mongoose," a well-financed, Miami-based venture to undermine the Cuban government through sabotage plots. Not only did the existence of such an operation show Kennedy to have been petty, vindictive, and obsessed with proving his *cojónes* against Castro's, but it also undermined the notion that the Bay of Pigs had prompted Kennedy's "growth" in office. If anything, Operation Mongoose showed Kennedy to have been as much of a cold warrior and hard liner after the bungled invasion of Cuba as before it.[22]

The most important question here, of course, is how much the revelations of the mid-1970s affected the public perception of JFK. Judged by some of the evidence, they seemed to shift the whole level of analysis to a lower plane; it was as if the epistemology of the *New York Times* and the *Washington Post* had been replaced by that of the *National Enquirer* and *People* magazine. Camelot, it seemed, could never again appear to be the pristine place its celebrants had claimed—there were simply too many Mafia dons and party girls dwelling within its precincts. The blurring of the private and public worlds the Kennedys had consciously sought to effect was completed in the revelatory literature, but in precisely the opposite way from what the Kennedys had hoped. Major matters of government policy, which had once seemed to hinge upon momentous questions of ideology and principle, were now seen as originating in the president's concupiscence and vanity. Ever since 1975 even serious scholarly studies have had to assess the impact upon Kennedy's policies of his love affairs, the Mafia, and the macho obsession with bringing down Castro.[23]

But the most salient aspect of the revelations was their lack of lasting impact on the Kennedy image. There has, in fact, been something of a case of national amnesia about them—a 1983 poll showed that relatively small percentages of Americans associated JFK with sexual misconduct in the White House or with plots to kill foreign leaders.[24] Even in the midst of the outpouring of revelations about Kennedy's private life, the most common public response seems to have been blasé. Perhaps, in a period of widespread cynicism and distrust, many Americans needed a symbol—no matter how tarnished—to cling to for reassurance. Perhaps, too, in an era that prided itself on its sexual sophistication, many were actually pleased or titillated at having had a "swinging" president. The Kennedy image had always appealed most to that kind of American who prided himself (or herself) on being liberated from bourgeois restraints and who probably laughingly agreed with Shirley MacLaine's oft-quoted remark that she preferred a president who did it to women to one who did it to the country. The favorite glib cliché of the Kennedy defenders, however, was that JFK's private life was only a fit subject for discussion insofar as it may have affected the conduct of his office.[25]

This last argument struck some as hypocritical. What, they asked rightly, of the Kennedys' confusion of private and public life? As they observed, it was the Kennedys who had paraded themselves as "role models" for the country. And, they asked, was it not part of the Kennedy appeal that one could be *chic* and *au courant*, yet also respect the family pieties? Since JFK had tried to make political capital out of his wife and children, was not the press right to inquire whether he had really been a good husband and family man? And what, after all, about the issue of *character*? The word had an old-fashioned ring, but character had been the ultimate basis of JFK's claims to superiority over other politicians.[26] These questions may not have much influenced the public image of JFK, but they have affected both the press's treatment of, and the public's attitudes toward, the Kennedys. Stung by all the evidence that JFK had been treated indulgently, the news media and journalists have eagerly sought to ferret out the less savory aspects of the Kennedy clan. Ted Kennedy's presidential candidacy in 1980 was dogged by stories about Chappaquiddick and sexual misconduct, while pieces about the arrogance and misbehavior of the younger Kennedys have become staples of the press.[27]

The revelations about Kennedy inevitably inspired a counterreaction. For the true believers in the JFK image, there was Theodore White's *In Search of History*. There, they could find the Camelot legend in all its pristine purity and majesty. White's Kennedy was the "clean and graceful" master-statesman of his age, who opened the gates of opportunity for non-WASPs, undermined "myths and fossil assumptions" in government, and brought a new style and a respect for intelligence to the government. The only "demerit" White gave Kennedy was for not imposing enough restraints on presidential power. But the burden of blame for this he placed on LBJ, "a man of boundless power appetite and reckless historical ambition" whom White blamed for all the problems of the late 1960s. As for Kennedy's infidelities, White simply shifted the onus of responsibility to the women involved: "Kennedy, the politician, exuded that musk odor of power which acts as an aphrodisiac to many women."[28]

White's defense of Kennedy, if it merits the word, simply side-stepped the major questions raised by the revelations of the mid-1970s. For a genuine effort of a Kennedy loyalist to grapple with those questions, one is better referred to the 1978 biography of Robert Kennedy by the ever-industrious Schlesinger. Schlesinger dismissed the rumors of a Kennedy-Monroe liaison with the statement that there was no substantial evidence of such an involvement, though one might demur that it is unlikely that the evidence of a clandestine love affair would meet the standard historical canons of reliability. On Campbell's calls to the White House, Schlesinger was simply sniffy: "One cannot conclude whether she was doing it out of a weakness for Presidents or whether she was put up to it by Giancana so that the underworld might get something on Kennedy. It seems improbable that she had a more complicated role."[29]

When Schlesinger turned to the revelations concerning Kennedy's foreign policy, he became incredible. He pointed to the lack of evidence that Kennedy knew of, or authorized, the CIA plots against Castro and suggested that either Eisenhower or Nixon may have originally authorized them. But this interpretation is damning for Kennedy, as it indicates that he had no control over an agency of his own administration. What is more, it does not take into account that the CIA had a policy of "plausible denial," under which presidents were able to imply acceptance of assassination plots without explicitly authorizing them. In light of this, the absence of written evidence of Kennedy's approval of the murder plots is irrelevant. Schlesinger also suggested that, as good Catholics, the Kennedys would not have condoned murder. There is no evidence, however, that religious scruples ever inhibited the Kennedys from ruthlessness toward a (real or perceived) foe. If anything, JFK prided himself on his lack of such scruples. Kennedy's "secret war" against Castro forced Schlesinger to engage in his most tortuous contortions of logic. He argued that Kennedy initiated Operation Mongoose not because he wanted to overthrow the Castro government but rather to halt its efforts to export revolution to Latin America. Pointing to Kennedy's feelers toward a normalization of relations with Cuba, he speculated that Kennedy was seeking a *quid pro quo* with Castro: the United States would accept the Cuban revolution in return for Castro's agreement not to spread unrest elsewhere in the Western Hemisphere.[30] This is an interesting thesis, but there is one problem with it: there is no evidence to support it.

One by-product of the revelations was intensified public demand for the reopening of the investigation into the Kennedy assassination. The exposure of the CIA-Mafia connections and the murder of Roselli shortly before he was scheduled to appear before the Church committee revived interest in conspiracy theories of Kennedy's murder. That interest was fed further by a new wave of books pointing to deficiencies in the official explanation of the assassination and suggesting possible involvement of the intelligence agencies and organized crime in JFK's killing and a subsequent cover-up.[31] Thus in September 1976 a special committee of the House of Representatives was created to investigate the murder of Kennedy, along with that of Martin Luther King, Jr. The committee met for two years, its final report being issued in January 1979. On the whole, its efforts were an exercise in bathos. It explored all the commonly suggested conspirators in the Kennedy assassination—the Kremlin, the Cuban government, right-wing Cuban exiles, the Mafia, the CIA, the FBI, and the Secret Service—and found no substantial evidence to implicate any of them. It did speculate, however, that individual Mafioso or Cuban exiles might have been involved. In the waning days of its deliberations, a majority of the committee voted to accept the validity of an experimental method of testing acoustical evidence that supported the theory that there had been a second gunman and thus "probably" a conspiracy to kill Kennedy. But this was more a tribute to the majority's eagerness to find a murder plot than to the strength of the new evidence. The experimental test on which the committee based its conclusion was of dubious validity, and its reliability was questioned by the FBI in 1980 and by the National Science Foundation in 1982.[32]

If the committee's deliberations were anticlimactic, so was the public's response. There was no wave of public indignation and no general outcry to find the possible conspirators in Kennedy's murder.[33] Perhaps the belief in a conspiracy was so widely held that the committee's findings came as no shock. Perhaps, too, the country was numbed by the revelations of ill-doing after Vietnam and Watergate and was not receptive to the prospect of prolonging the process of national purgation. It certainly seems to have been true that the political and polemical passions aroused by the literature of revisionism and revelation had abated somewhat by the late 1970s. This diminution of emotion was paralleled by the emergence of a more balanced and detached perspective on Kennedy, one that was most evident in scholarly studies of his life and legacy.

5 ■ Kennedy on Balance

In good part, the various images of JFK that have been discussed so far mirrored different phases in the self-conception of liberals. (Until recently, conservatives have not concerned themselves much with Kennedy.) The early postassassination image of JFK as the model of the modern, cosmopolitan president mirrored perfectly the outlook and values of "pragmatic" liberalism. Revisionism, of course, reflected a reaction against that outlook and those values and reflected also the ascendant intellectual influence of the New Left. But despite their serious interpretive disagreements, both Kennedy's liberal admirers and revisionist detractors shared a faith in the efficacy of an activist federal government to effectuate the public good. Seen in a historical perspective, that faith seems to have rested on a substratum of realities—most notably, the United States' preeminence in the post–World War II world and the general economic expansion and increasing affluence of the sixties and early seventies. Because of those conditions, liberals could more or less confidently expect (if not assume) that American power and largesse could be expended without substantial cost or injury to the public. But by the late 1970s, such realities no longer seemed to pertain. The underlying optimism and confidence (if not complacency) that had once characterized liberalism no longer seemed sustainable against a backdrop of shrinking resources (highlighted by the so-called "energy crisis"), blows to American prestige abroad, and the mushroom growth of federal entitlement programs with little demonstrable social impact. Against such a backdrop, some liberals began to reassess the limitations on the possibilities of purposive social change, inevitably with effects on their judgments of JFK's role in history.

The debate over liberalism's fate, and JFK's part in it, was supplied with a dramatic tableau: the official opening of the John F. Kennedy Memorial Library on October 21, 1979. The event had inherent drama, as two of the featured speakers were President Jimmy Carter and Senator Edward Kennedy, soon to become rivals for the Democratic presidential nomination. The venue was appropriate, too, for the story behind the protracted delay in opening the Kennedy library recapitulated, in many respects, the travails of American liberalism.[1] Like the New Frontier itself, the Kennedy library was launched with high hopes. In 1963 Kennedy had selected a site for the structure near the Harvard Business School, though he preferred a location at the repair yards of the Metropolitan Transit Authority (MTA), which were nearer Harvard Yard. Shortly after JFK's death, the Massachusetts state legislature yielded to the Kennedy family's wishes and agreed to purchase the site favored by the late president. But the Kennedys' plans, like JFK's centrist and elitist liberalism, ran afoul of the localist, "participatory" politics of the late 1960s and early 1970s. Community activists—led, ironically enough, by a Catholic priest and a black city councilwoman—helped block construction of the library at the MTA site, charging that it would attract chintzy souvenir shops, cause traffic congestion, and drive away poor residents by raising rents and property values. Finally, in 1975, strapped for funds and caught in lengthy court battles, the Kennedy Library Corporation withdrew its original plan. Soon afterward, it accepted an offer to build the library at Columbia Point in Boston, on landfill owned by the University of Massachusetts.[2]

But all these events were fading memories by the time of the opening ceremonies of the Kennedy library. An imposing, multi-winged structure of concrete and glass designed by I. M. Pei and Partners, the library seems to embody the boldness, confidence, and audacity of the Kennedy administration and its era in American history. But it suggests some of the subterranean realities of Camelot, too. Much of the exhibition space is underground, and a concrete tower houses confidential Kennedy manuscripts that will long remain closed to scholars.³ Of the two major antagonists at the dedication ceremony, Carter spoke first. Referring obliquely to Kennedy's soon-to-be-announced run for the presidential nomination, he reminded the audience of JFK's response at a 1962 press conference when asked if he would recommend his job to Ted or anyone else: "I do not recommend it to others—at least for a while." Inclining his head slightly toward Ted, Carter continued: "As you can well see, President Kennedy's wit, and also his wisdom, is certainly as relevant today as it was then." Having twitted Kennedy on his presidential aspirations, Carter turned to more serious concerns. He praised JFK for being a symbol of man's highest aspirations and recalled crying openly for the first time since his father's death when he heard news of Kennedy's assassination. But having honored the Kennedy legacy, he also reminded the audience that JFK had said that "change is the law of life." This observation allowed him to embrace one aspect of that legacy—JFK's sense of the limits of institutional life— yet also suggest that Kennedyite activism was inadequate to the challenges of the time:

> President Kennedy was right: change is the law of life. The world of 1980 is as different from what it was in 1960 as the world of 1960 was from that of 1940. . . . We have a keener appreciation of limits now; the limits of government, limits on the use of military power abroad; the limits of manipulating without harm to ourselves a delicate and a balanced natural environment. We are struggling with a profound transition from a time of abundance to a time of growing scarcity.⁴

Ted Kennedy followed. His remarks were an implicit call for the renewal of Kennedyite activism and confidence in mankind's capacity to shape the future. He recalled JFK as a man who "could make lightning strike on the things he cared about," and who called on governments to be as a "city upon a hill." He also suggested, by implication, that Carter's invocation of "limits" was contrary to JFK's faith in the power of positive leadership. In his peroration he tried to evoke the inspirational example of JFK with a succession of metaphors: "The spark still glows. The journey never ends. The dream shall never die."⁵

Although some—especially fervent admirers of the Kennedys— complained that Carter's retrospective commentary on Camelot was an easy rationale for the failures of his own leadership, the president's remarks seem to have captured a shift in the mood of many liberals. Even some Kennedy loyalists conceded that Carter had done well in his confrontation with Ted.[6] It may also be true that Carter's victories over Kennedy in the 1980 Democratic primaries marked a public recognition that inspirational activism and leadership were not enough to lead us out of difficulties.[7] No matter what the case, the recognition of limits on the capabilities of political leadership certainly had its parallel in scholarship on JFK in the middle and late 1970s. The development of such a new, more modest assessment of Kennedy's role was no doubt in good part due to a longer (if not necessarily better) sense of historical perspective on the Kennedy era. But to some degree, it also reflected a more sober estimate of the possibilities of positive social change on the part of liberal academics, intellectuals, and journalists. With their heightened appreciation of the complexities of the historical process, they could not see Kennedy as either the hero of the hagiographers or the villain of the revisionists. Rather, they saw him as a conventional, though somewhat imaginative, politician, whose behavior was shaped decisively (and not always consciously) by the prevailing social assumptions and institutions of his time.

To be sure, the keynote of the literature of "balance"—its attentiveness to how various realities imposed limits on Kennedy—was by no means new. Both Kennedy's liberal admirers and revisionist detractors had acknowledged some of the limits on Kennedy's freedom of action and maneuver. In the case of Kennedy's defenders, the recognition of "limits" had often served to explain or excuse JFK's hesitancy in tackling controversial issues. For example, they often ascribed Kennedy's unaggressive approach to the civil rights movement to his fear of alienating the southern Democratic bloc in Congress and of jeopardizing support for his initiatives in economic and foreign policy. By contrast, the revisionists, while conceding the existence of institutional pressures on Kennedy, had chided him, in effect, for not being imaginative and morally audacious enough to make new departures and educating the American people to follow his lead. However, the literature of balance made the conception of limits central to its interpretive framework. Kennedy the man figures prominently in it, but his role is clearly subordinated to that of the attitudes, ideas, and institutions within which he functioned. Its cumulative effect on Kennedy's image was not so much to change it as to diminish its proportions. Indeed, it is probably not too much to say that the literature of balance has been profoundly subversive of the main, underlying premise of almost all the preceding discussions of Kennedy—that he was the central, determinative force in the events of his era in American history.

[I]

As with the earlier literature on Kennedy, the scholarship of balance concentrated on issues of foreign policy. In this area, the balanced view of Kennedy incorporated elements of both the positive and the revisionist views. Like the adulatory Kennedy literature, it depicted JFK as, to some extent, a creative and dynamic leader. But it also scaled down the claims made for Kennedy's originality. Kennedy's "new ideas" themselves became simply typical of their time. Similarly, like the left revisionist interpretation of JFK, it portrayed him as an adherent (and perhaps even a captive) of cold war attitudes. But it simply accepted this as a historical datum rather than as a morally condemnatory judgment.

The pursuit of a balanced verdict is evident in Peter Wyden's study of the Bay of Pigs affair. In Wyden's view, Kennedy's role in that fiasco was an example of how an "assumed consensus" emerged from a process of "groupthink." Having inherited the project from the Eisenhower administration, Kennedy and his advisers feared to ask tough, probing questions because of the bureaucratic momentum behind it and their arrogant faith in their own luck and "vigor." Kennedy was also inclined to continue the scheme, Wyden reasoned, because of the Joint Chiefs' amenable attitude, which he misinterpreted as consent, rather than as willingness to go along with a project assumed to have the president's approval. General attitudes, unspoken and inarticulate, yet nevertheless pervasive, also had their effect. The reassuring faith that the Castro government was merely an imposition on an unwilling people lent plausibility to the idea that an exile landing would spark a popular revolt. There was also the "gook syndrome," which would later be painfully exhibited in Vietnam—the tendency to understate the "capabilities and determination" of non-Americans, especially those who were not white.[8]

Desmond Ball's study of the arms buildup under Kennedy similarly stresses the attitudinal and institutional factors that shaped Kennedy's decisions. While conceding that "ultimate responsibility" for the buildup lay with Kennedy, Ball made a persuasive case that bureaucratic "quasi-sovereignties" helped frame the alternatives presented to him. Each of those governmental forces—the military, the State Department, and the disarmament agency—had its own "strategic ideology" that determined its conception of how American interests could be served best. According to Ball, the fateful decision to accelerate American arms development even though there was no "missile gap" resulted from both institutional and personal factors—Kennedy's "haste" to improve the United States' strategic position and a "political compromise" between the rival institutional interests in the government. Ball reached a Scotch verdict on whether the arms buildup could have been avoided. He regretted its precipitancy as "unnecessary" but confessed that the internal politics behind the administration's arms policies were "perhaps inevitable."[9]

Another attempt to place Kennedy's nuclear policy within a historical framework may be found in Michael Mandelbaum's *The Nuclear Question*. Mandelbaum pointed to the profound degree of continuity in the essential aims of both Kennedy and Eisenhower through the deployment of nuclear weapons. Both maintained the same broad political commitments, upheld the doctrine of "deterrence," and supported the notion of "flexible response" because their policies were constrained, in good part, by ongoing political commitments and the nature of nuclear weapons and technology. The chief difference between the two administrations was one of "style." While Ike had been content to avow nuclear policy as a matter of "custom," the Kennedy strategists had made it "systematic, explicitly, and clear." For example, whereas Eisenhower had only "suggested" that the "survivability" of nuclear weapons was desirable, Kennedy *proclaimed* it as an objective of American policy. In Mandelbaum's view, the significance of the missile crisis was that it showed that deterrence could not prevent confrontations between the superpowers. The resulting test ban treaty tried to establish a "liberal world order" to limit the competition between the U.S. and the U.S.S.R., an objective that liberals had expected to emerge *eventually* from the operation of deterrence. The treaty was in this sense evidence of the "growth" of policy under Kennedy, but "growth" within the framework of established beliefs and preconceptions.[10]

Perhaps the most intelligent attempt at a balanced perspective on Kennedy's foreign policy is Herbert Dinerstein's study of the Cuban missile crisis. In this work, Dinerstein made a pioneering—though highly speculative—attempt to extract the motives of the Cubans and Russians from the available printed sources. His conclusions, though debatable, are noteworthy in that they suggest how the crisis may have grown out of unquestioned beliefs and assumptions on *both* sides. Castro, Kennedy, and Khrushchev were all, in Dinerstein's opinion, dominated in their thinking by preestablished "scenarios": Kennedy, by the domino theory and the fear of monolithic communism; Castro and Khrushchev, by the theory of spontaneous state conversion to communism. Like the left revisionists, Dinerstein argued that both Havana and Moscow genuinely feared a United States invasion of Cuba and believed the missiles would be a deterrent against such an attack. But Dinerstein also agreed with Kennedy's supporters that Khrushchev had self-serving motives for inserting rockets in Cuba: he wanted to improve the Soviet Union's standing in the arms race, augment his bargaining power in Berlin, and boost the Russian position in the Communist world vis-à-vis China. Dinerstein asserted that Khrushchev was also influenced by the belief that Kennedy had withheld support from the Bay of Pigs invasion out of fear of a war between the superpowers—a misapprehension that led him not to plan for the contingency that the United States would be unwilling to accept missiles ninety miles offshore.[11]

Dinerstein concluded that Kennedy, too, was influenced by a combination of motives. Kennedy accepted the "cogency" of the right wingers' argument that the Cuban missiles presented an ultimate (though not immediate) threat to U.S. power and prestige, and he used this argument to press for more vigorous action than "soft liners" such as Stevenson wanted. But Kennedy also genuinely feared the threat of nuclear war, and he used this danger to obtain the compliance of the hard liners to nonmilitary action. Dinerstein argued that both sides, acting from misconceptions and misapprehensions, "perhaps needlessly" frightened the world. But this was not merely the result of individual errors by Castro, Kennedy, and Khrushchev. Rather, it reflected the irrational dynamics of "deterrence," which required that both superpowers exploit the anxieties arising from the fear of massive retaliation to render the other more pliable.[12]

Inevitably, the scholarship of balance has addressed itself to the issue of Kennedy's moral responsibility for escalating the American role in Vietnam. Here, too, a notable waning of partisan passion and the aspiration toward an equitable assessment have had their effects.

Typically, the new scholarship on Vietnam has rejected as irrelevant, metaphysical, or simply unanswerable the question of what Kennedy might have done had he lived longer. Its concern has been to place Kennedy's decisions within the context of their times and to try to relate them to the later course of events. It has found that Kennedy's actions were bound and shaped by certain fundamental and unstated assumptions: the belief that communism was a monolithic force; the presumption that a non-Communist Vietnam was essential to American interests; and faith in the efficacy of American technology and "crisis management." The debate within the Kennedy administration between "hawks" and "doves," scholars have pointed out, was circumscribed by a consensus on these beliefs and was restricted almost exclusively to matters of method.[13]

Kennedy's policies, in turn, reflected both his administration's agreement on fundamentals and its disagreements over tactics. Like his advisers, Kennedy acted on the belief that South Vietnam was an important arena for the American fight against the advance of communism and one in which the United States' technological and military prowess could play a decisive role. But Kennedy's prosecution of the American involvement in Vietnam also mirrored aspects of the disparate advice he received from the "hawks" and "doves." On the one hand, Kennedy shared the desire of the "doves" to avoid a large-scale military commitment in Southeast Asia and saw the vital importance of the *political* side of the struggle in Vietnam. Hence he rejected requests for the insertion of U.S. combat troops and pressed the Diem regime for reforms. Kennedy also wanted to maintain his "options" in the war, which gave him more leverage with Diem. For this reason, he concealed the extent of the American role in Vietnam to avoid pressures from the public that might have limited his choices. On the other hand, Kennedy was anxious to avert a Communist takeover of South Vietnam and shared the belief of the "hawks" that American military aid would have to play an important part in blunting the aggressions of North Vietnam and the Vietcong. Thus he increased the number of American advisers over the Geneva limit, initiated covert operations against North Vietnam, and escalated his rhetoric on Vietnam to the point that the American people saw the conflict there as vital to the security interests of the United States.[14]

The ironic, unintended consequence of Kennedy's policies in Vietnam, according to the scholarship of balance, was that instead of *widening* his choices, they *narrowed* them. This was especially true after the meddling in the coup against Diem, which augmented the United States' psychological investment in the maintenance of a non-Communist South Vietnam. Furthermore, Kennedy's optimistic public assessments of the situation and his deceptions led the American people to think that the war could be won without heavy sacrifices of American men or materiel. Considered in the light of these facts, the administration's projection of a total withdrawal from Vietnam in 1965 was not, as Kennedy's admirers claimed, the result of a realistic judgment that the war was unwinnable. Rather, it was simply the continuation of a deceptive (and perhaps self-deluding) optimism about the prospects of South Vietnam's success against the Communist forces. LBJ, of course, inherited the Kennedy administration's fateful legacy of widening commitments and public misconceptions, and both his expansion of the war and his "credibility gap" can be seen as logical (if not inevitable) outcomes of policies that Kennedy had initiated.[15]

[II]

That a sensitivity to limits can decisively affect even a sympathetic view of Kennedy is evident in Carl Brauer's book on JFK's civil rights policies. In this work, JFK appears as neither the insensitive and timid politician of the revisionists, nor the innovative (though cautious) hero of the apologists. Rather, he appears as a moderate and somewhat conventional statesman, caught in the crosscurrents of his times and inhibited by many of the same beliefs that blinded most whites to the moral urgency of the black struggle for equality. Brauer pointed out that as a Democrat, Kennedy was caught between the need to assuage the southern wing of his party and his genuine desire to satisfy the aspirations of blacks. What is more, Kennedy feared that by alienating southern committee chairmen in Congress, he might harm the chance of passage of his domestic program. Kennedy also had a temperamental preference for working through elites, and he shared the prevailing view that Reconstruction after the Civil War had been a failure because it attempted to coerce southern whites into accepting changes in racial relations.[16]

As a consequence of his beliefs, Brauer observed, Kennedy first sought to emphasize the legal and institutional aspects of the federal fight against discrimination and segregation. This paradox of attempting to obtain fundamental reform through established leaders and institutions was reflected in Kennedy's judicial appointments policy: at the same time Kennedy was pleading with blacks to apply to the courts for redress, he deferred to segregationist congressmen when choosing federal judges in southern jurisdictions. It took repeated frustrations, culminating in the national trauma of Birmingham, to show Kennedy the depths of southern white resistance to desegregation and to open his eyes to the *moral* aspect of the black struggle for equality. This was "growth," to be sure, but not exactly of the kind seen by some of Kennedy's left-wing admirers. Kennedy's embrace of an omnibus civil rights bill had some profoundly *conservative* motives: concerned that the issues not be settled in the streets, he wanted to maintain control of the situation by channeling black outrage into constructive channels.[17]

Alan Shank has written a similar analysis of Kennedy's efforts to secure the passage of his entire domestic program. From the beginning of his administration, according to Shank, Kennedy felt that his freedom of action was limited by the narrow mandate he received in the 1960 election. Furthermore, Kennedy believed that congressional opinion on domestic issues was relatively fixed and immutable, and he feared that embracing such controversial causes as civil rights might endanger the rest of his program. Shank, to be certain, did criticize Kennedy for his inept leadership of even those programs he did support, such as federal aid to education and the creation of a cabinet-level Department of Housing and Urban Development. The important point about his book, however, is that it places Kennedy's leadership within a historical and institutional context. In fact, Shank's major conclusion is that cyclical shifts in public opinion are ultimately more important than personal presidential leadership in creating opportunities for the passage of federal programs.[18]

The concept of *self-imposed* limitations is central to Lewis Paper's largely favorable study of Kennedy's presidential leadership. To Paper, the chief paradox of the Kennedy administration was the disparity between the grand visions projected by the president's rhetoric and the paucity of his performance. Paper concluded that the public was "considerably blind" to the severity of the country's domestic problems in the early 1960s, but he also faulted Kennedy for failing to use the educational potential of his office. In Paper's opinion, this was the result of Kennedy's faulty assumptions about the nature of mass opinion and political leadership. Kennedy did not see that informing the public was a slow, gradual process requiring steady effort; he felt more comfortable exploiting dramatic foreign policy crises to mobilize the public. He was also apprehensive of the irrationality of mass opinion, feared the loss of support for his administration if it endorsed divisive measures, and was wary of the "political and economic uncertainties" that fundamental change might bring in its wake. The result of all this, in Paper's opinion, was a "frustrating" presidency that was "frozen in the past" and lacked "farsighted strategies" for dealing with problems. Kennedy's ideals were consequently compromised by his faulty "understanding of the American and international political system." Even more ominously, Kennedy's failure to educate the public on the need for, and costs of, reform meant that it was ill-prepared for the repercussions of his legislative proposals when they were passed under Johnson. For this reason, Kennedy was at least partly responsible for the racial turmoil and disillusionment with liberalism that came in the aftermath of his administration.[19]

Harris Wofford's *Of Kennedys and Kings* represents the most significant nonscholarly contribution to the literature of balance. This book is all the more interesting because it was written by a dedicated Kennedy loyalist—among other capacities, Wofford served as the head of Kennedy's civil rights division in the 1960 campaign. Wofford avowedly wrote the book to redress what he saw as the unduly harsh and antiheroic portrait of Kennedy drawn by the revisionists. Yet his defense conceded much to the Kennedy critics; Wofford described himself as "both committed and critical." To Wofford, the 1960s had a dual character, combining hope with violence, and the two murdered Kennedy brothers, along with Martin Luther King, Jr., were the "comic heroes" of the decade—"young, romantic, and over-reaching." Wofford saw this duality in the Kennedy record. He had no use for the swagger and arrogance of Kennedy's hard-line foreign policies or the pretensions of the "best and brightest." He was particularly rough on Kennedy for his "unregenerate" actions toward Cuba, though he did see some evidence of "growth" in Kennedy's reliance on nonmilitary advice during the missile crisis. Overall, Wofford condemned Kennedy's foreign policies for "haste" and "the false pragmatism that puts undue weight on the power of guns and dollars, and continued to let the fear of Communism—or the fear of seeming to be soft on Communism— distort if not dominate our world strategy." Wofford also granted that

Kennedy's civil rights policies may have been unduly cautious, though he also observed that "it may well be that the President was right, in the long run, to let things ripen as they did." But he also pointed to the brighter aspects of the New Frontier, especially its capacity to attract the idealism of young people through the Peace Corps.[20]

Wofford traced much of the mixed character of the New Frontier to the character of JFK himself:

> Politically, John Kennedy wanted to prove, as Alexander Hamilton proposed in the First Federalist paper, that Americans by their conduct and example can demonstrate that they are capable of governing themselves out of reflection and choice and need not to be forever governed by accident and force. But he never expected to get all he wanted, and he learned to live cheerfully—perhaps too cheerfully—with the continuing tension between what we are and what we ought to be. He encouraged the country to do the same.[21]

[III]

In some respects, the "balanced" view of Kennedy represents an important advance over previous interpretations. Above all, it constitutes a serious attempt to rescue Kennedy from anachronistic judgments and contemporary controversies; it does not try to appropriate him for or against a "cause." In terms of intellectual sophistication, it also has its attractions. With its sense of historical perspective and of the complexity of motivations and influences at work in situations, it is certainly preferable to some of the simpler interpretations that preceded it. Yet it also has the demerits of its advantages. All too often, the pursuit of a "balanced" verdict degenerated into an inability or unwillingness to make intellectual or moral discriminations. When all facts and opinions are accorded equal weight and worth, the scholar can plead "objectivity" as an excuse for his failure to render moral judgments on the evidence. For much the same reason, the scholarship of "balance" often has a centrist ideological bias; because its proponents disdained supposedly emotional and polemical judgments on Kennedy, they often confused the "objective" pursuit of truth with a view taken from an allegedly "neutral" or "detached" perspective.

The literature of "balance" also provokes, though often without addressing, the issue of personal responsibility. With their cultivated sense of the complex institutional forces and motivations at work in the decision-making process, its authors often failed to reckon with the simple fact that institutions and ideas are manipulable human constructs, not inert things, which impose their imperatives on people's behavior. This error is especially evident in the most serious problem of the "balanced" interpretations of the Kennedy presidency—the utter failure of "limits" as an *explanatory* device. An appreciation of historical circumstances is indeed necessary to understand the alternatives presented to, considered by, or even imaginable by, the actors in a given situation. But ultimately, it cannot tell us why they *chose* to act as they did. Thus the literature of "balance" cannot satisfactorily account for Kennedy's response to the Cuban missile crisis, the civil rights movement, or any of the other major challenges of his administration. In such matters, values, objectives, and all the other things we subsume under conscious human "will" came into play as decisive, if not determinative, considerations.

With the premium it places on subtlety and complexity, the balanced perspective on Kennedy seems well on its way to establishing itself as the prevailing mode of analysis in the academy. But its insights are too complex and refined for mass consumption or ready use in political polemics. The major medium for diffusing its findings will probably be the textbook, which is hardly an effective medium for either the communication or propagation of ideas.[22] Furthermore, the adoption of a balanced image of Kennedy would require a drastic downward revision of his importance in history. As the next chapter will show, American public opinion—as reflected in best-selling books, the broadcast media, mass circulation magazines, the popular press, and political rhetoric—continues to assume JFK's decisive importance in recent American history.

6 ■ Kennedy, Kennedy— and More Kennedy

Edward Kennedy's run for the Democratic presidential nomination in 1980 raised the ghosts of Camelot once again. Buoyed by high standings in the polls and the support of family friends and political retainers, the "Kennedy for President" campaign was launched with all the ballyhoo of a restoration. But as many observers saw, the very legends from which Ted Kennedy hoped to prosper helped contribute to his undoing. It was his misfortune to suffer from nearly two decades' reexamination of the Kennedy image. The press, stung by charges of being unduly favorable to the Kennedys in the past, scoured Ted's private life relentlessly, and some of its members implied that his candidacy was just more evidence of the Kennedy's arrogance and presumptuousness. When Ted failed to define a positive vision for the country in his now-famous interview with Roger Mudd, he was only following a preset script, for JFK's pledge to get the country moving again had been at least as vacuous as Ted's promise to give the country a better sense of direction. Yet Ted, unlike JFK, was widely criticized by the press and public. Kennedy's troubles were further compounded when President Carter showed in the Iranian hostage situation that the Kennedys had no monopoly of skill at the art of "crisis management."[1]

Thus what had begun in tragedy in 1963 seemed to end, in 1980, in farce. Shadowed by disappointed expectations, the Ted Kennedy campaign quickly degenerated into a grim effort to salvage vindication for the Kennedy image. Vindication—though of an ambiguous sort—did come eventually, but only after Ted was no longer a candidate. At the Democratic convention, Kennedy delivered one of the most brilliant speeches of his career, one that compelled the Carter delegates to yield on several contested platform planks. But by calling attention to the major unsolved problems of the Carter years, the speech reminded the public of the arguments Ronald Reagan would later use to unseat Jimmy Carter. Once again, Kennedy charisma helped undermine the Democratic party and an incumbent Democratic president.[2]

Ted's unsuccessful candidacy in 1980 prompted some observers to write of "the death of Camelot" or "an end to the Kennedy period in American politics." But such reports, like those of Mark Twain's demise, were somewhat exaggerated. If anything, the 1980 race showed the continued appeal of the JFK image in the public imagination. Ted, of course, had no choice but to run on the family name; it was, after all, his chief political asset. But it was also something of a liability. Invariably, even his best showings on the stump would disappoint voters who judged him not by some normal standard of comparison, but against the mythical status of his dead brothers. When measured against the exalted stuff of the Kennedy image, his leadership seemed uninspirational, his rhetoric, platitudinous, and his humor, witless. Even all the attention to Ted's private life did not prompt much reexamination of the JFK image; voters apparently found that they could safely condemn the darker aspects of the family legacy by striking at Ted while they continued to canonize his murdered brother.[3]

[I]

In tribute to the continuing fascination with JFK, the years surrounding the twentieth anniversary of his slaying prompted a new wave of articles, books, and television programs. But anyone looking for fresh insights and perspectives was bound to be disappointed. As John Gregory Dunne complained, "there are no new facts about the Kennedys, only new attitudes."[4] Even this judgment was probably too charitable, for the new works on JFK and the Kennedys mostly conformed to preestablished formulas. There were, of course, the predictable coffee table productions, in which the visually inclined could find pictorial confirmation of their cherished memories of Camelot.[5] A new "revelatory" book appeared, this one by the Kennedy family chauffeur, who repeated the hackneyed cliché that the Kennedys were "stage actors" who had become trapped by their public image.[6] Those who despaired of a Camelot restoration led by Ted could peruse a family authorized collective biography of the younger Kennedys, Shrivers, and Smiths that detailed the dynastic qualifications of the coming generation.[7] But like several earlier attempts at image shaping by the Kennedys, this volume was dogged by damaging revelations. In 1983 Robert F. Kennedy, Jr., was arrested in South Dakota for heroin possession, and in 1984, David Kennedy—presented in the book as a model recovered addict—died in Florida of a drug overdose.[8]

Those who did not want to face such disquieting news could draw sustenance from William Manchester's *One Brief Shining Moment*. It is difficult not to see this book as Manchester's extended *mea culpa* for his previous travails with the Kennedy clan. It retells the Camelot saga in hushed tones of reverence—the inscription is a quotation from Thomas Malory's *Le Morte d'Arthur*. But pietas is purchased at the expense of fidelity to the truth. *One Brief Shining Moment* unwittingly confirms that the JFK image can only be preserved by resolutely refusing to face the facts. Manchester wrote as if two decades of scholarship and revelations did not exist. Judith Campbell, Sam Giancana, and Operation Mongoose are never mentioned. Instead, Manchester reassured us that Kennedy was the master leader of his time, the witty and intellectual aristocrat who would have rescued us from our difficulties. According to Manchester, Kennedy would have pulled us out of Vietnam, begun détente with the Soviet Union, normalized relations with China and Cuba, and generally brought us closer to the millennium. It is an ingratiating vision, which Manchester repeated with almost childlike faith. But in his devotion, Manchester bordered almost on sacrilege; despite the references to King Arthur, "his" Kennedy was really the Christ of the modern era, who died for all our sins.[9]

Readers in search of more "balanced" approaches to Kennedy could turn to Herbert Parmet's two-volume biography and Ralph Martin's *A Hero for Our Times*. To class these books together may seem unfair, for they are, in important respects, quite different. Parmet's study is serious, well-researched, and scholarly, whereas Martin's book is an odd amalgam of puffery and sensationalism, culled mostly from readily available sources. But both authors tried to pursue an objective of "balance," which they confused with moral neutrality. As in Bradlee's *Conversations with Kennedy*, there is a peculiar dissociation between facts and values in their books. Martin adduced considerable evidence of Kennedy's compulsive promiscuity but avoided drawing the damning conclusions that seem to follow from it. He even seemed to imply at one point that Jacqueline had come to understand and perhaps even approve of JFK's womanizing.[10] When he turned to Kennedy's public life, Martin simply repeated the standard apologia. His Kennedy was the witty, life-affirming, and ever-growing aristocrat who was, as his title says, the hero of our times. Martin's only contribution to the standard view was more "evidence" that Kennedy intended to pull American troops out of Vietnam in 1965—in this case, a conversation Kennedy supposedly had with one of his aides, Larry Newman.[11]

The dissociation between facts and values is even more painfully apparent in Parmet's volumes because they aspire to be taken seriously as works of historical scholarship. Parmet reveals in full proportion the disturbing disparity between the private reality and the public appearance of the JFK image. Parmet's books are full of damning and well-researched findings. He documented JFK's many—and often indiscreet—love affairs; Joseph Kennedy, Sr.'s large role in securing the publication of *Why England Slept* in a version considerably reworked by Arthur Krock; JFK's merely tutelary role in the writing of *Profiles in Courage*; the long and close relationship between Kennedy and Joseph McCarthy; that Kennedy could easily have had his vote recorded in favor of the censure of McCarthy; and JFK's numerous but well-concealed health problems. Parmet's assiduous researches also lent scholarly support to the notion that the FBI's files on JFK's affairs with Inga Arvad and Judith Campbell may have made Kennedy unduly deferential to J. Edgar Hoover.[12] Yet Parmet seldom drew larger conclusions from all these findings. In fact, the schema of his biography conforms for the most part to the conventional saga of "growth." "His" Kennedy started out as a timid extension of his father and gradually matured into an independent force in his own right. To be sure, Parmet rejected some of the more extravagant claims of the proponents of the growth thesis, particularly with respect to Vietnam. Neither did his Kennedy depart much from the dogmas of the cold war, though Parmet saw this as no grounds for criticism, as Kennedy was only reflecting the prevailing views of his time. But his Kennedy did outgrow the confinements of his sheltered upbringing to attain at least partly the ideal of enlightened Whig leadership he early projected for himself.[13]

The most intellectually substantial contribution to the Kennedy literature of the early 1980s is Garry Wills's *The Kennedy Imprisonment*. Like much of Wills's work, this is not a scholarly book, but an idiosyncratic and sometimes brilliant mix of impressionistic journalism and serious social criticism. It is not the product of original research or especially original in its conclusions, though Wills's relentless tone might lead one to think so. For evidence, it leans heavily on the Blairs and Parmet, while its analysis of Kennedy's policies owes much to revisionism, and its discussion of Kennedy "charisma" is influenced considerably by Henry Fairlie and Victor Navasky. It also carries over from the revisionist canon a tendency toward hyperbole and the inversion of myths; Wills's critique of the Kennedys serves as a sounding board for an attack on the mendacity of modern American society.[14]

The argument of *The Kennedy Imprisonment* is built on the metaphor of its title. In Wills's view, the Kennedys have entrapped themselves in the Procrustean corruptions of wealth, power, sex, charisma, and image. The chief agency of the Kennedy sons' imprisonment was the family patriarch, from whom they acquired their predatory sexual ethics, compulsive competitiveness, and tendency to divorce appearances and reality. Joe Kennedy, Sr.'s teaching— much of it by example—bred men who were emotionally crippled in their dealings with others (especially women), preoccupied with proving their masculinity in public life, and driven obsessively to conceal their inner emptiness behind pleasant "images." And since concealment has been vital to advancing the family's political fortunes, the Kennedys, Wills argued, have made themselves prisoners of those who knew the reality behind the facades. Wills thus agreed with Parmet that JFK was beholden to J. Edgar Hoover because of the FBI director's information on his more indiscreet affairs. Wills also suggested that Robert Kennedy was restrained in his criticism of LBJ by the knowledge that the president had damaging information on the plots against Castro.[15]

All this, of course, is not new, though Wills's argument is more impressive coming from his skilled pen than a synoptic statement might make it appear. The most striking part of *The Kennedy Im-*

prisonment is the discussion of the role of "charisma" in sustaining the Kennedys' influence. Wills used the word not in the debased sense of common parlance, but in its Weberian meaning—to denote the attribute of leaders whose authority is derived from personal qualities of character rather than the law or tradition. According to Wills, the Kennedys have bestowed their personal "charisma" on their followers to create a "charismatic aristocracy" of "honorary Kennedys" who will do the family's bidding. Government servants in this family retinue have often lost touch with the mystique of legality and bureaucracy. Men of ideas have similarly lost their capacity for independence when in service to the Kennedys—"Camelot was the opium of the intellectuals." What is more, Wills argued, the Kennedys' reliance on charisma was so effective that the presidents following JFK felt compelled to rely on extrabureaucratic modes of authority. LBJ and Nixon were in fact so suspicious of the federal bureaucracy that they both created personal, extralegal cohorts to do their bidding. Eventually, the abuses committed by these "charismatic retinues," especially in the Watergate scandal, spread distrust of the government among the people themselves. Wills saw the ultimate delegitimization of the federal bureaucracy in Ronald Reagan's call to get government off the backs of the people—an ironic tribute to the erosion of confidence in public institutions begun by Kennedy.[16]

As the previous discussion indicates, the disparity between the private "reality" and public "image" of the Kennedys has become a central theme of contemporary discussions of JFK. Since the Kennedys have asserted their claim as a dynastic *family*, it was almost inevitable that this theme should find expression in the genre of domestic melodrama. *The Kennedys: An American Drama* by Peter Collier and David Horowitz[17] and *The Kennedys: Dynasty and Disaster, 1848–1983* by John H. Davis[18] are two recent volumes in what promises to be a growing number of works in this new literary medium. These books are largely in the revelatory mode—both are based extensively on confidential interviews—and their avowed purpose is to penetrate the imposing domestic mythology that has shielded the Kennedy family from public scrutiny. Like Wills's book, they, too, portray a family imprisoned by a straitjacket of moral compromises and compulsions. The idea of course has become a cliché, and in both volumes the Kennedys bear disturbing similarities to the demonic families of such prime-time soap operas as "Dallas" and "Dynasty." With respect to JFK, neither says much that is genuinely original. In both, he appears lacking in emotional depth of intellectual commitment, compulsively driven to prove his machismo, and recklessly and insatiably ambitious to the point that he compromised both himself and his country.[19] Metaphors and moralizing swallow up the man, who, in turn, is little more than the inverted self of the public "image." The most rewarding parts of the Collier and Horowitz book, significantly, are those about the younger Kennedys, whose own modes of self-destructiveness— drugs, alcohol, sex, and petty criminality—the authors imply, may be taken as fair warnings for those who would plot Kennedy restorations in the future.[20]

[II]

The twentieth anniversary of JFK's death prompted re- newed debate over the meaning of his life and legacy. But for the most part, this controversy was an encounter between long-estab- lished positions. Left-wingers dutifully repeated the hallowed shib- boleths that Kennedy was a dangerous cold warrior in foreign policy and a timid conservative in domestic affairs. Contrariwise, Ken- nedy's admirers tried to rescue him from such criticism with the familiar arguments that he was hampered by the conservative major- ity in Congress and was growing beyond a simple, bipolar view of the world at the time of his death. More, they pointed out defensively, there was "no evidence" that Kennedy authorized the assassination of Castro or even knew of the plots against the Cuban dictator.[21] The only interesting development was the attempt of several Kennedy loyalists to claim JFK as a model for Democrats dissatisfied with the state of their party and of liberalism in the early 1980s. Theodore H. White anticipated some of the lineaments of this argument in 1978 in his *In Search of History*. This book is in good part a lament for the degeneration (as White saw it) of liberalism from a philosophy of opportunity into one of entitlements. But White salvaged Kennedy from responsibility for this process with the curious claim that he was "more conservative" than his Democratic successors in the White House, Johnson and Carter.[22]

Theodore C. Sorensen advanced a related point of view in an article that in effect tried to claim JFK as a precursor of 1980s "neoliberals" who were attempting to dissociate their party from charges that it was fiscally irresponsible and "soft on communism." According to Sorensen, Kennedy could serve as a model for contemporary Democrats because he was emancipated from rigid ideological dogmas. Unlike the right-wingers, Sorensen wrote, JFK had believed in the temperate use of military force abroad and had been skeptical about the Pentagon's requests for first-strike weapons. But unlike reflexive left-wingers, he had also believed in the doctrine of deterrence, criticized leaders in the Third World, and had been a "fiscal conservative."[23] Sorensen's zeal to connect Kennedy's "pragmatic" liberalism with the "neoliberalism" of the 1980s may perhaps be seen in his championship of the presidential candidacy of Gary Hart, who was sometimes trumpeted as a neoliberal reincarnation of John Kennedy.

Although the debate over JFK continued to rage twenty years after his death, the public's adulatory image of him seems to have remained placidly unaffected by it. The most substantial evidence of this came in a Gallup poll commissioned by *Newsweek* magazine for its issue commemorating the twentieth anniversary of the assassination. Unremarkably, the poll found that Kennedy was by far the most popular American president. Thirty percent of those surveyed said that he was their first choice to be president at the present time. FDR, the second favorite, received only 10 percent. The poll also showed that overwhelming majorities of the respondents associated Kennedy with concern for working people and the poor, civil rights, activism, youth, a hard line toward the Soviets, glamour, and "style." Relatively small percentages connected Kennedy with race riots, abuses by the CIA, and sexual misconduct in the White House. Sixty-five percent of those questioned believed that the United States would be "much different" if he had not been killed, and 66 percent thought that he would have spent more money on the poor. Responses to only two of the questions marred the almost uniformly favorable portrait. The respondents split almost evenly on whether Kennedy would have gotten the U.S. more deeply involved in Vietnam (37 percent yes, 40 percent no), and a plurality (44 percent) believed that the alienation of young people in the sixties would have occurred even if Kennedy had not been assassinated.[24]

Like most polls, the *Newsweek*-Gallup survey had serious deficiencies. It did not ask probing questions, it did not inquire into the intensity with which views were held, and it did not indicate the extent of information on which the respondents' answers were

based. It probably said as much about Americans' appalling ignorance of their country's history as it did about their attitudes toward
presidents. In the poll, Carter and Reagan received approximately the
same positive ratings as Washington and Lincoln![25] But the cumulative results of the poll are disturbing, for they indicate an almost
childish faith in the wonder-working powers of presidential leadership. The image of Kennedy that emerges from the poll is not merely
heroic, it is almost messianic; it is of a Kennedy who would simulta-
neously have spent more on the poor, faced down the Russians,
helped harmonize the races, and infused the country with goodwill
and "style." One need not agree with Nancy Gager Clinch's dubious
psychohistorical speculations to agree with her that the popular
perception of JFK—which is confirmed by the poll—has elements of
regressive fantasy in it.[26] Lest this view appear exaggerated, one only
need examine the 1984 presidential election to see the magical public appeal of the Kennedy image.

[III]

The struggle over the JFK image in 1984 began with the
Democratic primary race. Since Ted had withdrawn from consideration, no major contestant could assert special custodianship of the
Kennedy legacy. John Glenn, who had close personal ties to the
Kennedy family and had literally rocketed to fame during the presidency of JFK, perhaps had the strongest claim.[27] But of all the Democratic rivals, Gary Hart seems to have been perceived by the public as
fitting the Kennedy mold best. Like JFK, he was youthful and attractive—as was his wife—and he appealed self-consciously to a "new
generation" of Americans impatient with established party leaders
and institutions. Like JFK, Hart, too, based his candidacy on the
intangibles of "style"; by his own admission, he had few substantive
disagreements with Walter Mondale.[28] The similarity helped carry
Hart far, but not far enough. Many were wary of media-made candidates, especially one as synthetic as Hart, who had changed his name
and signature and whose positions were so indefinable in conventional ideological terms that he was alternately described as a liberal,
neoliberal, conservative, and pragmatist. It was only appropriate,
then, that Hart, himself so much the product of image making, had
his pretensions to being the candidate of "new ideas" punctured by
an advertising slogan.

But the most suggestive use of Kennedy's name in the 1984 campaign was not by a Democrat, but by such Republicans (and ex-Democrats) as Ronald Reagan and Jeanne Kirkpatrick. Along with assorted conservatives and "neoconservatives," they used the name of JFK (and those of FDR and Truman) to appeal to Democrats disaffected by their party's emphasis on the "limits" of American capabilities and who shared Reagan's more traditional confidence in the efficacy of American power and prestige. Ted Kennedy and other Democrats, of course, howled at this sacrilege.[29] But the Republicans were only paying a backhanded (or should one say right-handed?) compliment to the Kennedy hagiographers' success at elevating their hero to near-mythic status. Like Jefferson and Lincoln before him, Kennedy had become the property of the whole country—and both parties.[30] More to the point, it was Kennedy's admirers who had made much of the intangibles in Kennedy's appeal, and there was something disingenuous about their attempts to claim Kennedy for a single party or point of view. They missed the point altogether when they protested that JFK would not have voted for Reagan or endorsed his positions on arms control, foreign policy, and social security.[31] This was true, but quite irrelevant in the public perception. On the grounds of intangibles, there were indeed deep similarities between the appeals of Kennedy and Reagan. Both rose to the presidency bewailing the decline of national greatness and promising to get the country moving again; both exploited widespread popular distrust of government and promised to restore American greatness through personalized leadership, bypassing a flaccid and unresponsive bureaucracy; most important of all, both promised a restoration of national vitality and preeminence without compelling Americans to reckon the costs. (In this regard, the tax cuts championed by both men are highly emblematic of the similarities between them.)[32]

With the appropriation of Kennedy's name by conservative Republicans, the appeal of the JFK image would seem to have transcended politics. If Kennedy could be claimed by both parties and men with widely dissimilar views, then what meaning, one might well ask, did his legacy really have? This was, of course, precisely the significance of the Republicans' invocations of Kennedy in 1984; as Reagan intuitively realized, the JFK image appealed to vague emotions and sentiments, not to any specific set of beliefs or ideology. Thus, while there will no doubt be new interpretations of Kennedy, tailored to changing intellectual fashions and sensibilities, there is good reason to doubt that they will have much effect on the popular perception of JFK. Still, the easy use of the Kennedy image for conservative purposes should serve as a warning to those who genuinely believe in the need for purposeful social change. For to continue to nurture any of the mutations of that image would be to perpetuate a delusion subversive of intellectual honesty and a realistic assessment of the challenges that lie ahead of us.

7 ■ Afterword

The preceding pages have provided a schematic chronological survey of certain prevalent American images of John F. Kennedy that have emerged since his death. The analysis therein suggests that those images have arisen as the result of changes in the
country's intellectual, political, and social life. The image of Kennedy that had greatest currency after the assassination was shaped
mostly by northeastern elites (including the deceased president's
family) and reflected the "pragmatic" liberalism that was intellectually fashionable in the early 1960s. In brief, this image depicted JFK
as the ideal personification of the values of cultural modernism and
instrumental rationality. In this conception, he had been a uniquely
"autonomous" and dynamic leader, emancipated from "irrational"
prejudices and preconceptions, who had been destined to lead the
United States away from complacency and provincialism and to
prepare it for an "Augustan" age of cultural and political ascendancy
in the world. From the perspective of those creating this image, the
Kennedy assassination had almost totemic significance: it was the
sacrificial offering of the prince of Camelot to the forces of bigotry,
irrationality, and fanaticism. There were, of course, dissenting views
of Kennedy in the immediate aftermath of the assassination. But
they were mostly expressed—at least articulately and overtly—by

men and women at the margins of the political spectrum and of virtually no political consequence.

The revisionist view of Kennedy, of course, took shape in reaction against the perceived failures of American liberalism. Rather than seeing Kennedy as an invigorating break with the past, revisionists depicted him as a cleverly stylized and somewhat updated adherent of conventional assumptions and attitudes. JFK's chief failure as a leader, they argued, was precisely that he failed to question (or did not question in sufficient depth) the underlying premises of American politics in his time—the cold war against communism, faith in the beneficence of corporate capitalism and technology, and gradualism in social policy. What he did contribute to American politics and policy, in the revisionists' view, was a sophistication of technique and a grandiloquence of rhetoric that often had disastrous results, particularly in the country's relations abroad.

The revelations of the mid-1970s had a complex effect on the Kennedy image. On the one hand, they seemed to lend credence to the revisionist critique of JFK as a cold warrior with a compulsion to prove his masculinity. On the other, by obscuring the line between Kennedy's private and public lives, they reinforced the tendency— which was by no means new—to view JFK from the perspective of melodrama and soap opera—in effect, to trivialize him. The middle and late 1970s also saw the emergence of a more balanced and detached view of Kennedy, which was most evident in the scholarly literature on his presidency. This new image reflected the lengthening of historical perspective on the Kennedy presidency, as well as a heightened sensitivity among liberal intellectuals of the "limits" on the capacity for purposeful social change.

The chronological structure of the argument above might suggest that there has been a "development" or "evolution" of images of Kennedy. That conclusion would be erroneous. No "image" of Kennedy has supplanted the one preceding it, and all the modes of analyzing JFK—the orthodox liberal, revisionist, revelatory, and "balanced"—are evident in the contemporary debate over his place in history. Indeed, the wide variety of approaches is paralleled by a profusion of Kennedy "images," each suited to a particular audience. For conservatives and neoconservatives, there is Kennedy the hardline cold warrior, tax cutter, and advocate of national discipline; for leftists, there is Kennedy the incipient populist radical; for liberals, Kennedy the high-minded statesman; and for neoliberals, the tough and "realistic" politician whose prime virtue seems to have been simply that he was a Democrat who won elections.

In good part, JFK has become a congenial subject for the projection of disparate ideas and values because his own legacy and pronouncements represented a compound of imperatives that events have conspired to set in opposition. While he strove to release the energies of his countrymen, Kennedy also sought to maintain social discipline; while he admired the public stewardship of enlightened elites, he also exhorted the virtues of citizen activism; and while he vigorously asserted American power abroad, JFK also conceded its limitations. But the malleability of the Kennedy image to conflicting political purposes suggests as well that the public has been relatively unmoved by—if not impervious to—the protracted debate over JFK. It certainly reinforces the finding of the polls that the public's admiring image of JFK transcends ideology and has flourished in spite of—if not because of—popular ignorance of his life and achievements. Beyond this largely negative assessment, however, the polls are not very helpful in determining what the public does admire in Kennedy. In the absence of more concrete evidence, one might be tempted to speculate about Kennedy's subconscious role in the American psyche. But a "psychohistorical" analysis of this sort would rest on dubious assumptions about the collective unconscious—itself a highly questionable concept.[1] A more sensible and modest line of inquiry, though one that can only be suggestive, draws one's attention to the role of "images" in mass consumer culture.[2] For the Kennedy image, which has certainly become something of a commodity, exhibits some of the chief traits of the "images" disseminated by advertisers for popular consumption. In the Kennedy image, one also sees projected fantasies of omnipotence and wish fulfillment and the illusion that it is possible to make choices without consequences and commitments.[3] That consumer images have no specific ideological content is wholly consistent with the underlying intellectual vacuity—and hence infinite adapatability—of the popular Kennedy image.

While the Kennedy image mirrors some aspects of modern consumer society, it also seems to derive much of its popularity from ideas and ideals deeply ingrained in American culture. The "eternally young" Kennedy, rescued by premature death from the inevitable ravages and disillusionments of age, has become a symbol of how many Americans have traditionally seen their country—as one of boundless hope and promise, free of the burdens and limits of the past. It is not without significance that the "New Frontier" label has become firmly attached to the Kennedy era, even though JFK himself hated it. That the actualities of the Kennedy administration were quite discordant with such an image only serves to show that symbols often embody needs that render literal facts irrelevant.

These reflections may easily lead one to pessimistic conclusions about the prospects of propagating a more realistic view of JFK and of generally raising the level of popular political thought in the United States. But as Freud himself suggested, fantasies may have a positive value when they are brought into the light of day, as they may contribute to rational insight into our less rational selves. Thus the highest value of an inquiry into our collective images of so widely admired a figure as JFK may be that it will contribute to a better understanding of how we see—or, rather, would like to see—ourselves.

NOTES

1. Introduction

1. Tom Shachtman, *Decade of Shocks: Dallas to Watergate, 1963–1974* (New York, 1983). The popular sense that the Kennedy assassination was a violent rupture in American history is also apparent in some of the interviews quoted in Peter Goldman, "Kennedy Remembered," *Newsweek*, Nov. 28, 1983, pp. 61–66, 75–78, 83–84, 86, 91.

2. " . . . And a Child's Yellow Flowers," *Newsweek*, Dec. 2, 1963, pp. 36–37; Wilbur Schramm, "Communication in Crisis," in Bradley S. Greenberg and Edwin B. Parker, eds., *The Kennedy Assassination and the American Public: Social Communication in Crisis* (Stanford, 1965), 3, 19; Fred I. Greenstein, "College Students' Reactions to the Assassination," ibid., 223–27.

3. Tom Wicker, *JFK and LBJ: The Influence of Personality upon Politics* (New York, 1968), 159; Vance Bourjaily, *The Man Who Knew Kennedy* (New York, 1967), 33; Louis Harris, *The Anguish of Change* (New York, 1973), 171.

4. Paul B. Sheatsly and Jacob J. Feldman, "A National Survey on Public Reactions and Behavior," in Greenberg and Parker, eds., *Kennedy Assassination*, 154–55; Charles M. Bonjean, Richard J. Hill, and Harry W. Martin, "Reactions to the Assassination in Dallas," ibid., 190–92; Roberta S. Sigel, "Television and Reactions of Schoolchildren to the Assassination," ibid., 210–12; Martha Wolfenstein and Gilbert Kliman, eds., *Children and the Death of a President* (Garden City, 1965), 190. By contrast, the members of groups that did not strongly identify with Kennedy—southern whites, Protestants, and Republicans—tended to react less emotionally to the assassination and usually compared it to a traumatic historical event such as Pearl Harbor.

5. Schramm, "Communication in Crisis," 23; James D. Barber, "Peer Group Discussion and Recovery from the Kennedy Assassination," in Greenberg and Parker, eds., *Kennedy Assassination*, 115–17. For more information on psychological responses to the assassination, see J. Ahler and J. Tamney, "Some Functions of Religious Ritual in a Catastrophe: Kennedy Assassination," *Sociological Analysis* 25 (1964): 212–30; Stephen A. Appelbaum, "The Kennedy Assassination," *Psychoanalytic Review* 53 (Fall 1966):69–80; Thomas J. Banta, "The Kennedy Assassination: Early Thoughts and Emotions," *Public Opinion Quarterly* 28 (1964): 216–24; and George R. Krupp, "The Day the President Died: Its Meaning and Impact," *Redbook*, March 1964, pp. 49, 98–104. The most complete account of the Kennedy funeral is William Manchester, *Death of a President* (New York, 1967), chap. 9.

6. Aubrey Mayhew, *The World's Tribute to John F. Kennedy in Medallic Art* (New York, 1966); Edward C. Rochette, *The Medallic Portraits of John F. Kennedy (A Study of Kennediana). With Historical and Cultural Notes and a Descriptive Catalogue of the Coins, Medals, Tokens and Store Cards Struck in His Name* (Iola, Wis., 1966). In the United States alone, Kennedy's likeness was placed on a new fifty cent piece, a seventy-five dollar savings bond, and a commemorative stamp.

7. Anne Chamberlin, "The Commercialization of J.F.K.," *Saturday Evening Post*, Nov. 21, 1964, pp. 20–21; T. M. Gannon, "Kennedy Memorabilia," *America*, Sept. 19, 1964, pp. 304–306; "Memorial Boom," *Newsweek*, Dec. 30, 1963, pp. 49–50.

8. Among the best and most tasteful of such works are Laura Bergquist, *A Very Special President* (New York, 1965); McFadden-Bertell Co., *A John F. Kennedy Memorial, by the Editors, McFadden-Bertell Company* (New York, 1964); NBC News, *There Was a President* (New York, 1966); *New York Times, The Kennedy Years* (New York, 1964); Doris E. Saunders, ed., *The Kennedy Years and the Negro: A Photographic Record* (New York, 1964); Mark Shaw, *The John F. Kennedys: A Family Album* (New York, 1964); Tazewell Shepard, Jr., *John F. Kennedy: Man of the Sea* (New York, 1965); Tony Spina, *This Was the President: Text and Photos* (New York, 1964); and United Press International and Chase Studios, Ltd., *John F. Kennedy: From Childhood to Martyrdom* (Washington, 1963).

9. For a listing of such recordings, see Martin H. Sable, *A Bio-Bibliography of the Kennedy Family* (Metuchen, N.J., 1969), 226–28. See also Carlton Brown, "The Kennedy Memorial Albums," *Redbook*, July 1964, p. 30; and Herbert Kupferberg, "Kennedy Memorial Albums," *Atlantic*, April 1964, pp. 134, 136–37.

10. "Land of Kennedy: Renaming of Plazas, Bridges, Parks, Etc.," *Time*, Dec. 13, 1963, p. 27; "And Then It Was November 22 Again," *Newsweek*, Nov. 30, 1964, p. 26.

11. Significantly, attempts to name public structures after Kennedy were usually unsuccessful when they became embroiled in politics. For example, a movement to rename the Verrazano-Narrows Bridge after JFK was blocked by opposition from Italian American organizations. The renaming of Cape Canaveral, which was imposed by President Lyndon B. Johnson, aroused opposition among local residents; the original name was restored in 1973, by which time the emotions connected with Kennedy's assassination had begun to diminish somewhat.

12. See the huge number of works on the assassination listed in DeLloyd J. Guth and David R. Wrone, comps., *The Assassination of John F. Kennedy: A Comprehensive Historical and Legal Bibliography, 1963–1979* (Westport, 1980); and William Clifton Thompson, *A Bibliography of Literature relating to the Assassination of President John F. Kennedy* (San Antonio, 1968).

13. The massive proportions of the Kennedy literature are evident in such bibliographies as William H. Carr, *JFK: A Complete Bibliography, 1917–1963* (New York, 1964); James Tracy Crown, *The Kennedy Literature: A Bibliographical Essay* (New York, 1968); Joan I. Newcomb, *John F. Kennedy: An Annotated Bibliography* (Metuchen, N.J., 1977); Dorothy Ryan and Louis J. Ryan, eds., *The Kennedy Family of Massachusetts: A Bibliography* (Westport, 1981); Sable, *Bio-Bibliography of the Kennedy Family*; and Ralph A. Stone, ed., *John F. Kennedy, 1917–1963: Chronology—Documents—Bibliographical Aids* (Dobbs Ferry, N.Y., 1971). There are also nu-

merous entries on Kennedy in such reference guides as *The Reader's Guide to Periodical Literature; Biography Index; Essay and General Literature Index; Social Science and Humanities Index;* and *Public Affairs Information Service Index.*

14. Witness, for example, the various uses of "myth" and "legend" in such works as Joseph Campbell, *The Hero with a Thousand Faces,* 2d ed. (Princeton, 1968); Marshall W. Fishwick, *American Heroes: Myth and Reality* (Washington, 1954); Orrin E. Klapp, *Heroes, Villains, and Fools: The Changing American Character* (Englewood Cliffs, 1962); and Lord Raglan, *The Hero: A Study in Tradition, Myth and Drama* (London, 1936). The various (and often ambiguous) uses of the "myth" concept by members of the American Studies movement in the 1950s prompted a large, controversial literature that need not be discussed here. But for an example, see Barry Marks, "The Concept of Myth in *Virgin Land,*" *American Quarterly* 5 (Spring 1953): 71–76. Because of the scholarly controversy over the meaning of "myth," it has largely been dropped from American historical discourse.

15. Daniel J. Boorstin, *The Image: or, What Happened to the American Dream* (New York, 1962).

16. Orrin E. Klapp, *Symbolic Leaders: Public Dramas and Public Men* (Chicago, 1964), 27–29. For interpretations of the shifting perceptions of Kennedy that differ from those advanced in the present work, see Donald C. Lord, *John F. Kennedy: The Politics of Confrontation and Conciliation* (Woodbury, N.Y., 1977), chap. 8; and Vincent L. Toscano, *Since Dallas: Images of John F. Kennedy in Popular and Scholarly Literature, 1963–1973* (San Francisco, 1978).

17. This has been pointed out in John Hellmann, *American Myth and the Legacy of Vietnam* (New York, 1986), 223.

2. The Image Created

1. For some of Robert Kennedy's uses of John Kennedy's name, see the quotations reprinted in Douglas Ross, *Robert F. Kennedy: Apostle of Change* (New York, 1968), 9, 14, 24, 44, 302, 335, 337, 374, 381–83, 416–17, 441, 471, 492, 497. See also "What's Bobby to Do—An Informal Talk with RFK," *Newsweek,* July 6, 1964, pp. 24–25; Penn Kimball, *Bobby Kennedy and the New Politics* (Englewood Cliffs, 1968), *passim;* and William V. Shannon, *The Heir Apparent: Robert Kennedy and the Struggle for Power* (New York, 1967), *passim.*

2. Edward Kennedy invoked JFK in his first speech after RFK's assassination (*New York Times,* Aug. 22, 1968, p. 22) and in his infamous address to the people of Massachusetts after the Chappaquiddick incident, in which he admitted speculating after the accident whether "some awful curse did actually hang over all the Kennedys" (ibid., July 26, 1969, p. 10). See also James McGregor Burns, *Edward Kennedy and the Camelot Legacy* (New York, 1976); Theo Lippman, Jr., *Senator Ted Kennedy* (New York, 1976), esp. 72, 147, 183; and Robert Sherrill, *The Last Kennedy* (New York, 1976), 55–56, 222.

3. "Camelot Censored?" *Newsweek,* Oct. 3, 1966, p. 65; Andy Logan, "JFK: The Stained-Glass Image," *American Heritage,* Aug. 1967, pp. 6–7, 75–78.

4. For the fullest account of the Manchester imbroglio, see John Corry, *The Manchester Affair* (New York, 1967), esp. 67, 99–100, 126, 128, 142, 147,

112 ■ Notes to pages 8–9

182, 183, 222–23. See also "Camelot Censored?" 65–66; "The Presidency: Battle of the Book," *Time*, Dec. 23, 1966, pp. 15–18; "Growing Rift of LBJ and Kennedys," *U.S. News and World Report*, Jan. 2, 1967, pp. 22–27; Kimball, *Bobby Kennedy*, 55–57; Shannon, *Heir Apparent*, 256–83. The Manchester-Kennedy accord is reprinted in *New York Times*, Jan. 17, 1967, p. 25.

5. For example, LBJ used JFK's name three times in his first State of the Union address (*New York Times*, Jan. 9, 1964, p. 33) and paid warm tribute to his memory during a campaign stop at Boston (ibid., Oct. 28, 1964, p. 33). Doris Kearns's remarks on Johnson's references to Kennedy during the transition period are perceptive: "The living President armed himself with the passionate admiration, intensified by his death, that many felt for John Kennedy and with the still unfulfilled goals of the Kennedy administration. By carrying out what his predecessor had started, Johnson argued that his call to continue was in effect John Kennedy's call. Johnson was but the 'dutiful executor' of his predecessor's will. Throughout the transition period the slain President was invoked, in a powerful and decisive fashion. In the early weeks and months after the assassination, Johnson's public addresses were filled with allusions to John Kennedy." Doris Kearns, *Lyndon Johnson and the American Dream* (New York, 1976), 179. Once Johnson was elected in his own right, his references to JFK diminished in number and frequency.

6. There was a particularly flagrant example of the partisan use of Kennedy's name in the 1964 elections. Hubert H. Humphrey, the Democratic vice presidential candidate, suggested that the voters of Ohio could make up for their state's rejection of JFK in 1960 by voting the Democratic ticket in 1964. This story is retold in Malcolm Muggeridge, "The Apotheosis of John F. Kennedy," *New York Review of Books*, Jan. 28, 1965, p. 2.

7. For Kennedy's symbolic role in boosting Catholic self-esteem, see Lawrence H. Fuchs, *John F. Kennedy and American Catholicism* (New York, 1967), 31, 164–68, 201, 229, 235–37. See also John Cogley, "Kennedy the Catholic," *Commonweal*, Jan. 10, 1964, pp. 422–24; Albert J. Menendez, *John F. Kennedy: Catholic and Humanist* (Buffalo, n.d.); and William V. Shannon, *The American Irish* (New York, 1964), chap. 19.

8. "Ebony Photo-Editorial: A Tribute to John F. Kennedy," *Ebony*, Jan. 1964, pp. 90–91; Carl T. Rowan, "How Kennedy's Concern for Negroes Led to His Death," ibid., Feb. 1964, pp. 17–19; Harry L. Golden, *Mr. Kennedy and the Negroes* (New York, 1964); *Moral Crisis: The Case for Civil Rights, as Stated by John F. Kennedy* [and others] (Minneapolis, 1964).

9. The most important writers who shaped the Kennedy image were Joseph Alsop, Benjamin Bradlee, Joseph Kraft, James Reston, Richard Rovere, Hugh Sidey, Theodore White, and Tom Wicker. This list, of course, is far from exhaustive.

10. "Current Comment: Climate of Hate," *America*, Dec. 14, 1963, p. 758; *San Francisco Chronicle*, Nov. 26, 1963, p. 36; "Hatred Breeds Fanaticism," *Des Moines Register*, Nov. 26, 1963, p. 8; Sue Reinert, "Dallas, Long a Radicals' Haven," *New York Herald-Tribune*, Nov. 23, 1963, p. 8. The "climate of hate" argument inspired a protracted national debate that can be followed in *New York Times*, Nov. 25, 1963, pp. 5, 10; ibid., Nov. 28, 1963, pp. 26, 27; ibid., Dec. 2, 1963, pp. 16, 40; ibid., Dec. 9, 1963, p. 38. Conservatives, of course, rejected the accusations of collective responsibility for the assassination. Not only did such accusations conflict with their ideological preconceptions, but also it was a source of satisfaction for them that the

assassination was officially blamed on a Marxist. See "The Good People of Dallas," *Chicago Tribune*, Nov. 26, 1964, p. 16; "John F. Kennedy," *Dallas Morning News*, Nov. 23, 1963, p. 4; "The Week: JFK, 1917–1963," *National Review*, Dec. 10, 1963, p. 1; Statement of House of Representatives Republican Policy Committee, *New York Times*, Dec. 7, 1963, p. 12; Thurston B. Morton, "Collective Guilt? A Senator's Answer," *U.S. News and World Report*, Dec. 23, 1963. p. 74; and the statements of Senators McClellan, Eastland, and Johnston in U.S. Congress, *Memorial Addresses in the Congress of the United States and Tributes in Eulogy of John Fitzgerald Kennedy, Late a President of the United States . . .* (Washington, 1964), 50–52.

11. "America Weeps," *Chicago Sun-Times*, Nov. 23, 1963, p. 7; Doris Fleeson, "The Forces of Hate," *New York Post*, Nov. 26, 1963, p. 30; Ralph Emerson McGill, "Hate Knows No Direction," *Saturday Evening Post*, Dec. 14, 1963, pp. 8, 10; "John F. Kennedy: A Symbolic Warning," *St. Louis Post-Dispatch*, Nov. 23, 1963, p. 8-A; Eric Sevareid quoted in "The Meaning of the Life and Death of John F. Kennedy," *Current*, Jan. 1964, pp. 18–19.

12. Ben Bagdikian, "The Assassin," *Saturday Evening Post*, Dec. 14, 1963, p. 22; Frederick D. Kershner, Jr., and Anthony F. C. Wallace quoted in "Meaning of the Life and Death of John F. Kennedy," 20–21. Aspects of all three of the arguments outlined here were advanced in Walter Lippmann, "Murder Most Foul," *New York Herald-Tribune*, Nov. 26, 1963, p. 30.

13. John Cogley, "Death of the President," *Commonweal*, Dec. 6, 1963, p. 299; H. Stuart Hughes, "A Most Unstuffy Man," *Nation*, Dec. 14, 1963, p. 409; James Reston, "Why America Weeps," *New York Times*, Nov. 23, 1963, pp. 1, 7; Theodore C. Sorensen, *Kennedy* (New York, 1965), 46–47, 750.

14. Cogley, "Death of the President," 299; Hughes, "Most Unstuffy Man," 409; Arthur M. Schlesinger, Jr., *A Thousand Days: John F. Kennedy in the White House* (Greenwich, Conn., 1965), 664–65; Sorensen, *Kennedy*, 750.

15. Joseph Kraft, *Profiles in Power: A Washington Insight* (New York, 1966), 8.

16. "Significance in History," *New Leader*, Dec. 9, 1963, p. 4.

17. Schlesinger, *Thousand Days*, 668.

18. This story (which of course was not widely known in 1963) was later retold in David Halberstam, *The Best and the Brightest* (New York, 1972), 4. For Kennedy's courtship of intellectuals in 1960 and during his administration, see Schlesinger, *Thousand Days*, 35–36; and Sorensen, *Kennedy*, 117–18, 176, 230, 251–54, 384–86.

19. Richard Hofstadter, *Anti-Intellectualism in American Life* (New York, 1963), 227–28.

20. Schlesinger, *Thousand Days*, 109.

21. John Cogley, "JFK: A Final Word," *Commonweal*, May 8, 1964, pp. 190–91.

22. Arthur M. Schlesinger, Jr., "The Administration and the Left," *New Statesman*, Feb. 8, 1963, p. 185; Arthur M. Schlesinger, Jr., *The Vital Center* (Boston, 1962).

23. Roger Hilsman, *To Move a Nation: The Politics of Foreign Policy in the Administration of John F. Kennedy* (Garden City, 1967), 47; Richard H. Rovere, "Notes and Comment," *New Yorker*, Nov. 30, 1963, p. 52; Schlesinger, *Thousand Days*, 103–105; Sorensen, *Kennedy*, 386; Theodore C. Sorensen, *The Kennedy Legacy* (New York, 1969), 166–67.

24. R. Jeffrey Lustig, *Corporate Liberalism: The Origins of Modern*

American Political Theory, 1890–1920 (Berkeley, 1982), 1–4, 6–10, 158, 169–70, 191–94.

25. On this theme, see Robert Booth Fowler, *Believing Skeptics: American Political Intellectuals, 1945–1964* (Westport, 1978), esp. 3–4, 121–42, 167, 189–91; and Marian J. Morton, *The Terrors of Ideological Politics: Liberal Historians in a Conservative Mood* (Cleveland, 1972).

26. Theodore H. White, *The Making of the President, 1964* (New York, 1965), 19–20.

27. John P. Roche, "Kennedy and the Politics of Modernity," *New Leader*, Aug. 17, 1964, pp. 7–13; Schlesinger, *Thousand Days*, 677–95.

28. Roche, "Kennedy and the Politics of Modernity," 13.

29. Schlesinger, *Thousand Days*, 21, 111–14, 279–80, 287, 353, 467–76, 914–16, 925. See also Roche, "Kennedy and the Politics of Modernity," 12; Sorensen, *Kennedy*, 21–23, 333–36, 510–11, 537–40; and Sorensen, *Kennedy Legacy*, 238–40.

30. This was most obvious in White's description of Kennedy's intellectual "court." See White, *Making of the President, 1964*, 21.

31. For such a view, see Christopher Lasch, "The Life of Kennedy's Death," *Harper's*, Oct. 1983, pp. 32–40.

32. Samuel Eliot Morison, "John Fitzgerald Kennedy, 1917–1963: A Eulogy," *Atlantic*, Feb. 1964, p. 49. For another expression of such elitist snobbery, see Pearl S. Buck, *The Kennedy Women: A Personal Appraisal* (New York, 1970).

33. Joseph Alsop, "The Legacy of John F. Kennedy: Memories of an Uncommon Man," *Saturday Evening Post*, Nov. 21, 1964, p. 16.

34. John William Ward, "John F. Kennedy: The Meaning of Courage," in John William Ward, *Red, White and Blue: Men, Books, and Ideas in American Culture* (New York, 1969), 149. On the intellectual atmosphere in the United States in the late 1950s and early 1960s, see William E. Leuchtenburg, *A Troubled Feast: American Society since 1945* (Boston, 1973), 108–18; and Allen J. Matusow, *The Unraveling of America: A History of Liberalism in the 1960s* (New York, 1984), chap. 1.

35. Tom Wicker, "Lyndon Johnson versus the Ghost of Jack Kennedy," *Esquire*, Nov. 1965, p. 158.

36. Schlesinger, *Thousand Days*, 114.

37. Ibid., 616.

38. William Attwood, "In Memory of John F. Kennedy," *Look*, Dec. 31, 1963, p. 2; Fletcher Knebel, "The Unknown JFK," ibid., Nov. 17, 1964, p. 50; Kraft, *Profiles in Power*, 3; Sorensen, *Kennedy*, 24.

39. Rovere, "Notes and Comment," 53. See also Sorensen, *Kennedy Legacy*, 154; and Tom Wicker, *Kennedy without Tears: The Man beneath the Myth* (New York, 1964), 43.

40. James MacGregor Burns, "The Legacy of 1,000 Days," *New York Times Magazine*, Dec. 1, 1963, pp. 27, 118, 120; William G. Carleton, "Kennedy in History," *Antioch Review* 24 (Fall 1964): 296–97; Morison, "John Fitzgerald Kennedy," 48; Sorensen, *Kennedy*, 389, 757; White, *Making of the President, 1964*, 36.

41. Schlesinger, *Thousand Days*, 668. For more on Kennedy's wit, see Kraft, *Profiles in Power*, 3; Kenneth P. O'Donnell and David F. Powers with Joe McCarthy, *"Johnny, We Hardly Knew Ye": Memories of John Fitzgerald Kennedy* (Boston, 1972), 406; and Sorensen, *Kennedy*, 6, 62–63.

42. On the "new politics," see especially Kimball, *Bobby Kennedy*, pas-

sim. See also Robert Westbrook, "Politics as Consumption: Managing the Modern American Election," in Richard Wightman Fox and T. J. Jackson Lears, eds., *The Culture of Consumption: Critical Essays in American History, 1880–1980* (New York, 1983), 145–73.

43. Eric F. Goldman, *The Tragedy of Lyndon Johnson* (New York, 1969), 16–17.

44. One may dispute Christopher Lasch's characterization of the "narcissistic" personality, but his description of the role of fantasy in modern life would seem to be relevant here: "The mass media, with their cult of celebrity and their attempt to surround it with glamor and excitement, have made America a nation of fans, moviegoers. The media give substance to and thus intensify narcissistic dreams of fame and glory, encourage the common man to identify with the stars and to hate 'the herd,' and make it more and more difficult for him to accept the banality of everyday existence." Christopher Lasch, *The Culture of Narcissism: American Life in an Age of Diminishing Expectations* (New York, 1979), 55–56.

45. Sorensen, *Kennedy*, 387–88; Rovere, "Notes and Comment," 53. See also Wicker, *Kennedy without Tears*, 43–44.

46. Daniel Bell, *The Cultural Contradictions of Capitalism,* (New York, 1976), 44, describes the emergence of "middlebrow culture" in the 1950s: "In effect, culture, as it came to be conceived in the mass middle-class magazines, was not a discussion of serious works of art, but a style of life that was organized and 'consumed.' Following suit, cultural criticism became a snob's game, played by advertising men, magazine illustrators, home decorators, women's magazine editors, and East Side homosexuals as one more fashionable amusement."

47. Norman Mailer, "After Kennedy's Death," in Norman Mailer, *The Idol and the Octopus* (New York, 1968), 241.

48. Schlesinger, *Thousand Days*, 669. For more tributes to Kennedy's "style," see Benjamin Bradlee, "He Had That Special Grace," *Newsweek*, Dec. 2, 1963, p. 38; Carleton, "Kennedy in History," 296–97; Cogley, "JFK: A Final Word," 191; Kraft, *Profiles in Power*, 8; Reinhold Niebuhr, "A Tentative Assessment," *New Leader*, Dec. 9, 1963, p. 7; Arthur M. Schlesinger, Jr., "A Eulogy: John Fitzgerald Kennedy," *Saturday Evening Post*, Dec. 14, 1963, pp. 32–33; Sorensen, *Kennedy*, 7, 61; White, *Making of the President, 1964*, 30, 218, 312, 330.

49. Schlesinger, *Thousand Days*, 92–94.

50. Mailer is quoted in Schlesinger, *Thousand Days*, 114.

51. Max Weber, "Politics as a Vocation," in H. H. Gerth and C. Wright Mills, trans. and ed., *From Max Weber: Essays in Sociology* (New York, 1958), 115–25.

52. Schlesinger, *Thousand Days*, 113. See also ibid., 79–98, 112–15.

53. Sorensen, *Kennedy*, 14.

54. James David Barber, *The Presidential Character: Predicting Performance in the White House* (Englewood Cliffs, 1972), 318; O'Donnell and Powers, "Johnny," 406; Sorensen, *Kennedy*, 6.

55. Pierre Salinger, *With Kennedy* (Garden City, 1966), 121, 323–25; Schlesinger, *Thousand Days*, 658–59; Sorensen, *Kennedy*, 4, 311–26.

56. Paul B. Fay, Jr., *The Pleasure of His Company* (New York, 1966), 36–37.

57. Ibid., 102. For more stories indicating Kennedy's preoccupation with his image, see ibid., 35, 95, 100, 196, 202–203, 208.

58. Barber, *Presidential Character*, 314–15; Kimball, *Bobby Kennedy*, 32–34; Schlesinger, *Thousand Days*, 609, 678–79; Shannon, *Heir Apparent*, 249–50. For some astute comments on the glorification of youth in the 1960s, see Kenneth Crawford, "The Youth Myth," *Newsweek*, Nov. 7, 1966, p. 36; Shannon, *Heir Apparent*, 244–45, 247.

59. For a history of this agency from a pro-Kennedy, anti-Johnson viewpoint, see Daniel Knapp and Kenneth Polk, *Scouting the War on Poverty: Social Reform Politics in the Kennedy Administration* (Lexington, Mass., 1971).

60. Victor S. Navasky, *Kennedy Justice* (New York, 1971), 331. See also Sorensen, *Kennedy Legacy*, 81.

61. On the admiration of young people for JFK, see "An Ideal Man—They Remember JFK," *Newsweek*, March 22, 1965, p. 47; and B. T. Calvin Lee, *The Campus Scene: 1960–1970* (New York, 1970), chap. 6. Unfortunately, these (and similar) surveys of youth opinion in the 1960s are biased toward middle class, college-educated young people; we have relatively little information on the views of non-college-educated youth.

62. Edwin Guthman, *We Band of Brothers* (New York, 1971), 97–98. See also Kimball, *Bobby Kennedy*, 97–98; and O'Donnell and Powers, "*Johnny*," 73. Louis Harris recalled JFK telling him in the spring of 1960 that the "real significance" of his victory "will be that we will have by-passed a whole generation. Never again will anyone from Stevenson's generation be president. I think the establishment resents our youth as much as anything else. But it is time the vigor of youth took over." Louis Harris, *The Anguish of Change* (New York, 1973), 200.

63. For a discussion of the conflicts of generations in the 1960s, see Paul M. Kattenburg, *The Vietnam Trauma in American Foreign Policy, 1945–1975* (New York, 1980), 271–72. For some evidence of the class and cultural differences between the RFK and McCarthy constituencies, see "How the Voters See the Issues," *Newsweek*, March 25, 1968, p. 26; Jean Stein and George Plimpton, *American Journey: The Times of Robert Kennedy* (New York, 1970), 247.

64. Joseph Campbell, *The Hero with a Thousand Faces* (Princeton, 1968).

65. Barber, *Presidential Character*, 297–314; Carleton, "Kennedy in History," 279–80; Cogley, "Death of the President," 299; O'Donnell and Powers, "*Johnny*," 103–104, 137; Schlesinger, *Thousand Days*, chap. 4; Sorensen, *Kennedy*, 26–54; Sorensen, *Kennedy LEgacy*, 5–79; Wicker, *Kennedy without Tears*, 57–58, 60.

66. Schlesinger, *Thousand Days*, 892. See also Barber, *Presidential Character*, 319–42; Carleton, "Kennedy in History," 289–96; "Ebony Photo-Editorial: A Tribute to John F. Kennedy," 90; Fay, *Pleasure of His Company*, 191–92; Guthman, *We Band of Brothers*, 108, 114, 128; Robert F. Kennedy, *Thirteen Days: A Memoir of the Cuban Missile Crisis* (New York, 1971), 89–90, 95, 97, 102–104; O'Donnell and Powers, "*Johnny*," 277–78; Sorensen, *Kennedy*, 23–24, 294–309, 509, 752–53; Sorensen, *Kennedy Legacy*, 17, 79, 81, 87–89, 92–93, 180–82, 184–85, 187–89, 191–92, 218–20, 238–40, 247, 262, 265–68; James L. Sundquist, *Politics and Policy: The Eisenhower, Kennedy, Johnson Years* (Washington, 1968), 113; and White, *Making of the President, 1964*, 23–24, 85.

67. On this fallacy, see David Hackett Fischer, *Historians' Fallacies: Toward a Logic of Historical Thought* (New York, 1970), 15–21.

68. The fullest expressions of such speculation occur in the conspiratorial works discussed in the next two footnotes.

69. Portions of *MacBird!* were reprinted in *Ramparts*, and the play received a respectful reception from Dwight Macdonald and other left-wing critics. See the reviews and foreword appended to Barbara Garson, *MacBird!* (New York, 1967); and Dwight Macdonald, "Birds of America," *New York Review of Books*, Dec. 1, 1966, pp. 12, 14. *MacBird!* had a respectable run (379 performances) at New York's Village Gate and Garrick Theater. Jim Garrison's view of the assassination (and Johnson's role in it) is most clearly presented in his *A Heritage of Stone* (New York, 1970), esp. 28, 35, 51, 253. On Garrison's following, see Milton E. Brener, *The Garrison Case: A Study in the Abuse of Power* (New York, 1969); James Kirkwood, *American Grotesque: An Account of the Clay Shaw–Jim Garrison Affair in the City of New Orleans* (New York, 1970); and Gene Roberts, "The Case of Jim Garrison and Lee Oswald," *New York Times Magazine*, May 21, 1967, 32–35ff.

70. For such conspiracy theories, see Thomas G. Buchanan, *Who Killed Kennedy?* (New York, 1964) [right-wing oil men]; Alvin Gershenson, *Kennedy and Big Business* (Beverly Hills, 1964) [business magnates]; Joachim Joesten, *Oswald, Assassin or Fall Guy?* (New York, 1964) [the FBI and Dallas police]; Penn Jones, Jr., *Forgive My Grief*, 3 vols. (Midlothian, Tex, 1966–69) [Texas right-wingers and LBJ]; Harold Weisberg, *Whitewash: The Report on the Warren Report* (Hyattstown, Md., 1965), chap. 8 [Dallas police]; Harold Weisberg, *Oswald in New Orleans: Case for Conspiracy with the CIA* (New York, 1967) [CIA]; and Harold Weisberg, *Whitewash II: The FBI–Secret Service Cover-Up* (Hyattstown, Md., 1966) [FBI and Secret Service].

71. This was a common feeling immediately after the assassination. See Bradley S. Greenberg and Edwin B. Parker, eds., *The Kennedy Assassination and the American Public: Social Communication in Crisis* (Stanford, 1965), 128, 236; Martha Wolfenstein and Gilbert Kliman, eds., *Children and the Death of a President* (Garden City, 1965), 188.

72. In February 1971 she returned for the first time since December 1963 to observe the unveiling of portraits of herself and JFK. "Mrs. Onassis Returns for White House Visit," *New York Times*, Feb. 4, 1971, p. 19.

73. Goldman, *Tragedy of Lyndon Johnson*, 150, 164, 228; Henry Fairlie, "Johnson and the Intellectuals: A British View," *Commentary*, Oct. 1965, p. 49. See also "The Kennedy Legend and the Johnson Performance," *Time*, Nov. 26, 1965, pp. 30–31.

74. Wicker, "Lyndon Johnson," 156.

75. Jack Newfield, *Robert Kennedy: A Memoir* (New York, 1969), 169–88.

76. Schlesinger, *Thousand Days*, 939–40; Sundquist, *Politics and Policy*, 482–84; Richard Wilson, "What Happened to the Kennedy Program," *Look*, Nov. 17, 1964, pp. 117–21.

77. Guthman, *We Band of Brothers*, 28–29; Salinger, *With Kennedy*, 44–46; Schlesinger, *Thousand Days*, 45–61, 645–49; Sorensen, *Kennedy*, 162–67, 187–89, 213–19, 266–67.

78. Schlesinger, *Thousand Days*, 43.

79. Evelyn Lincoln, *Kennedy and Johnson* (New York, 1968), 147–49, 159, 183, 192, 205 (quotation).

80. O'Donnell and Powers, *"Johnny,"* 7, 192–93. For a slightly different version, see Kenneth P. O'Donnell, "LBJ and the Kennedys," *Life*, Aug. 7, 1970, pp. 33, 44–45. O'Donnell and Powers, however, rejected Lincoln's claim that Kennedy intended to drop LBJ in 1964. O'Donnell and Powers, *"Johnny,"* 5.

81. Sorensen, *Kennedy Legacy*, 34; Shannon, *Heir Apparent*, 6–8, 60. See

also Stein and Plimpton, *American Journey*, 128, 129; and Jules Witcover, *85 Days: The Last Campaign of Robert Kennedy* (New York, 1969), 329. For RFK's platform in 1968, see Ross, *Robert F. Kennedy*, 543, 547–48, 551–59, 576–93.

82. Ross, *Robert F. Kennedy*, 9, 14, 24, 25, 374, 381–83, 429, 441; Shannon, *Heir Apparent*, 7–8.

83. "What's Bobby to Do," 24.

84. Witcover, *85 Days*, 116, quoting a speech at the Greek Theater in Griffith Park, Los Angeles, March 24, 1968.

85. This was in a speech at Vanderbilt University, quoted in Witcover, *85 Days*, 109–10. RFK seems to have literally believed that a president could determine the tone and style of American life. When David Halberstam suggested to him that some of the country's divisions were not Johnson's fault, he replied: "I don't think so at all. I think the country wants to be led and needs to be led. I think it wants to do the right thing." David Halberstam, *The Unfinished Odyssey of Robert Kennedy* (New York, 1968), 93.

86. Victor S. Navasky, "The Haunting of Robert Kennedy," *New York Times Magazine*, June 2, 1968, pp. 26, 78. There are several versions of the McCarthy quotation; I have accepted the one quoted in this article.

87. Schlesinger, *Thousand Days*, 654.

88. Ibid., 288–89, 296, 414; Sorensen, *Kennedy*, chap. 22.

89. Sorensen, *Kennedy Legacy*, 186.

90. Hilsman, *To Lead a Nation*, chap. 25; Schlesinger, *Thousand Days*, 781–83, 796–805; Sorensen, *Kennedy*, 558–75.

91. Schlesinger, *Thousand Days*, chap. 21; Sorensen, *Kennedy*, 537–40.

92. Counterinsurgency will be discussed below, in the section on Kennedy and Vietnam.

93. W. W. Rostow, *The View from the Sixth Floor* (New York, 1964), 13–14, 26; Schlesinger, *Thousand Days*, 176–94, 529–32, 540–43, 547–65, 697–726; Sorensen, *Kennedy*, 533–37. Schlesinger confessed to misgivings about the "blandness" of the policy prescriptions based on the "stages of growth" theory, but conceded that they were probably the "best" the United States had to offer. Schlesinger, *Thousand Days*, 542–43.

94. Guthman, *We Band of Brothers*, 108, 114; Hilsman, *To Lead a Nation*, chap. 3; Schlesinger, *Thousand Days*, 210–15, chaps. 10–11; Sorensen, *Kennedy*, 295–309; Sorensen, *Kennedy Legacy*, 73–81, 271–80.

95. Schlesinger, *Thousand Days*, 336, 341, 353–64; Sorensen, *Kennedy*, 543–50, 583–601. O'Donnell and Powers claimed that Kennedy was not really prepared to go to war over Berlin but felt compelled to threaten to do so because of previous commitments. O'Donnell and Powers, *"Johnny,"* 291, 299–302.

96. Guthman, *We Band of Brothers*, 128; Kennedy, *Thirteen Days*, esp. 9, 14, 40, 63–64, 73–74, 94–97, 104; Hilsman, *To Lead a Nation*, chaps. 13–16; O'Donnell and Powers, *"Johnny,"* 310–18; Rostow, *View*, 10, 38; Schlesinger, *Thousand Days*, 728–29, 735–37, 759–61, 768–69, 815–36; Sorensen, *Kennedy*, chap. 24, pp. 729–33, 740–46; Sorensen, *Kennedy Legacy*, 187–88.

97. The most detailed analysis of Kennedy's economic policies from a favorable viewpoint is E. Ray Canterbery, *Economics on a New Frontier* (Belmont, Calif., 1968), esp. 3–4, 22–25, chap. 18. See also Walter Heller, *New Dimensions of Political Economy* (New York, 1967); Schlesinger, *Thousand Days*, chaps. 23–24; Sorensen, *Kennedy*, chaps. 16–17; and Sorensen, *Kennedy Legacy*, 237–38. For more objective accounts, see Seymour

Harris, *Economics of the Kennedy Years and a Look Ahead* (New York, 1964); Jim F. Heath, *John F. Kennedy and the Business Community* (Chicago, 1969); and Hobart Rowen, *The Free Enterprisers: Kennedy, Johnson, and the Business Establishment* (New York, 1964).

98. Sorensen, *Kennedy*, 470–472. See also Schlesinger, *Thousand Days*, chap. 35.

99. Schlesinger, *Thousand Days*, 849–57 (quotation at 849); Sorensen, *Kennedy*, 473–78.

100. Sorensen, *Kennedy Legacy*, 223; Schlesinger, *Thousand Days*, chap. 36 (quotation at 883); Sorensen, *Kennedy*, chap. 18 (quotation at 495–96).

101. Schlesinger, *Thousand Days*, 492.

102. Hilsman, *To Lead a Nation*, 28–33; Schlesinger, *Thousand Days*, 499–500, 503–509, 895–99; Sorensen, *Kennedy*, 648–61.

103. Schlesinger, *Thousand Days*, 909–10. See also ibid., 896, 900–909; Sorensen, *Kennedy*, 652–54, 658–60.

104. Sorensen, *Kennedy*, 661.

105. For LBJ's early conduct of the war, see Leslie H. Gelb with Richard K. Betts, *The Irony of Vietnam: The System Worked* (Washington, 1979), chap. 4; George C. Herring, *America's Longest War: The United States and Vietnam, 1950–1975* (New York, 1979), 108ff.; and Kattenburg, *Vietnam Trauma*, 122ff.

106. Guthman, *We Band of Brothers*, 318; Tom Wicker, "Kennedy and Johnson," *New York Times*, June 24, 1965, p. 16.

107. Robert Scheer, "A Political Portrait of Robert Kennedy," *Ramparts*, Feb. 1967, p. 16.

108. Halberstam is quoted in Stein and Plimpton, *American Journey*, 202. The Kennedys' enthusiasm for counterinsurgency is also discussed in Hilsman, *To Move a Nation*, 415–16, 425–26; Newfield, *Robert Kennedy*, 113; and Shannon, *Heir Apparent*, 112–13.

109. Hilsman, *To Move a Nation*, 532–34.

110. Arthur M. Schlesinger, Jr., *The Bitter Heritage: Vietnam and American Democracy, 1941–1966* (Boston, 1966), 1, 20, 23–24, 56–87, 99–102, 105–106.

111. Chester L. Cooper, *The Lost Crusade: America in Vietnam* (Greenwich, Conn., 1972), 417.

112. Clayton Fritchey, "A Tale of One City—and Two Men," *Harper's*, Dec. 1966, pp. 108–10.

113. Tom Wicker, *JFK and LBJ: The Influence of Personality upon Politics* (New York, 1968), 194–95.

114. Newfield, *Robert Kennedy*, 183, 224; Witcover, *85 Days*, 82.

115. See his remarks quoted in *New York Times*, Dec. 21, 1967, pp. 1, 27. For a more coherent version, see Ross, *Robert F. Kennedy*, 536–37.

116. Witcover, *85 Days*, 102, quoting a speech of March 18, 1968, at Kansas State University.

117. Mailer, "After Kennedy's Death," 278.

118. Henry Brandon, *Anatomy of Error: The Inside Story of the Asian War on the Potomac, 1954–1969* (Boston, 1969), 26, 28.

119. Sorensen, *Kennedy Legacy*, 204.

120. O'Donnell, "LBJ and the Kennedys," 51–52. This story is repeated in O'Donnell and Powers, *"Johnny,"* 16–17.

121. *New York Times*, Aug. 3, 1970, p. 16.

122. See Kearns, *Lyndon Johnson*, 263–64; and Gelb and Betts, *Irony of*

Vietnam, 196, 223, for Johnson's fears of a right-wing reaction. The O'Donnell story is repeated in Barber, *Presidential Character*, 32–33; William Manchester, *One Brief Shining Moment: Remembering Kennedy* (Boston, 1983), 223–25; and Theodore H. White, *In Search of History: A Personal Adventure* (New York, 1978), 530–31.

123. Gerald W. Johnson, "Once Touched by Romance," *New Republic*, Dec. 7, 1963, p. 15. Actually, however, Kennedy is far less of a true folk hero than another martyred president, Abraham Lincoln. Although Lincoln, too, had his "image makers," most of the extravagant stories and legends about him that gained currency after his death arose spontaneously from the people and thus can be said to have reflected popular dreams and aspirations. By contrast, the Kennedy "image" is far more of a synthetic creation, fabricated out of a veritable glut of information (and misinformation) supplied by the communications media. This may help explain why, for all its elements of fantasy, the Kennedy "image" lacks the imaginative depth and richness of the Lincoln "legend." See David Donald, *Lincoln Reconsidered* (New York, 1961), chap. 8; and Lloyd Lewis, *Myths after Lincoln* (New York, 1929).

124. Carleton, "Kennedy in History," 298–99.

125. William Manchester, *Death of a President* (New York, 1967), 623. Manchester's interpretation was influenced by Mary Renault [pseud.], *The King Must Die* (New York, 1958).

126. Marshall W. Fishwick, *The Hero, American Style* (New York, 1969), 11–12. Fishwick is influenced here by Lord Raglan, *The Hero: A Study in Tradition, Myth and Drama* (London, 1936).

127. Theodore H. White, "For President Kennedy: An Epilogue," *Life*, Dec. 6, 1963, p. 159. The lines, of course, are from the musical *Camelot*, with book and lyrics by Alan Jay Lerner and music by Frederick Loewe. For another evocation of "Camelot," see Rose Fitzgerald Kennedy, *Times to Remember* (Garden City, 1974), 112.

128. Kennedy's usual place in the legend is that of King Arthur; but sometimes he is Lancelot. For references to Kennedy in the latter role, see U.S. Congress, *Memorial Addresses*, 246, 299.

129. See, for examples, Lawrence F. O'Brien, *No Final Victories: A Life in Politics—From John F. Kennedy to Watergate* (Garden City, 1974), 147–48; and White, *In Search of History*, 525.

130. "We Want Camelot Again," *Newsweek*, March 25, 1968, p. 27.

131. See Bernard Bailyn, *The Ideological Origins of the American Revolution* (Cambridge, Mass., 1967).

132. Daniel Bell has quoted one of his Harvard colleagues who served in the Kennedy administration as saying, "We blew it. There was a challenge to create a sustained Establishment as in Britain, and it all went." Bell, *Cultural Contradictions*, 202. One story about Kennedy that bears similarity to the Arthurian legend holds that JFK was not assassinated but leads a life of mystery, sequestered away from the world. (There were similar stories about Arthur that foretold his ultimate restoration to the throne.) See Bruce A. Rosenberg, "Kennedy in Camelot: The Arthurian Legend in America," *Western Folklore* 35 (Jan. 1976): 52–59. Despite the patient absurdity of the story about Kennedy, it has had remarkable persistence in popular folklore, perhaps because of its undercurrents of wishful thinking.

133. White, *In Search of History*, 457. The heroic image of JFK is best preserved in the innumerable children's books that hold up Kennedy as a

model for American youth. These books may be partly responsible for Kennedy's enduring popularity with young people.

134. "Birch View of JFK," *Newsweek*, Feb. 24, 1964, pp. 29–30; Norbert Murray, *Legacy of an Assassination* (New York, 1964); Revilo P. Oliver [pseud.], "Marksmanship in Dallas; Part I," *American Opinion*, Feb. 1964, pp. 18–36; *idem*, "Marksmanship in Dallas: Part II," ibid., March 1964, pp. 22–47.

135. "The Week: JFK," 1; Thomas A. Lane, *The Leadership of President Kennedy* (Caldwell, Idaho, 1964); Malcolm E. Smith, *Kennedy's 13 Great Mistakes in the White House* (New York, 1968).

136. Carleton, "Kennedy in History," 256–58, 291; Wicker, *JFK and LBJ*, 84–89, 120–44.

137. Howe, quoted in "Kennedy and After," *New York Review of Books*, Dec. 26, 1963, p. 5; Milton Mayer, "November 22, 1963," *Progressive*, Dec. 1964, pp. 23–24; Carey McWilliams, "Kennedy Memorial Albums," *New York Herald-Tribune Book Week*, May 3, 1964, p. 15; Hans Morgenthau, "Monuments to Kennedy," *New York Review of Books*, Jan. 6, 1966, pp. 8–9.

138. "We All Had a Finger on That Trigger," in Neil Middleton, ed., *I. F. Stone's Weekly Reader* (New York, 1973), 166–70; I. F. Stone, "The Brink," *New York Review of Books*, April 14, 1966, pp. 12–15; I. F. Stone, "The Test Ban Comedy," ibid., May 7, 1970, pp. 13–21.

139. George Kateb, "Kennedy as Statesman," *Commentary*, June 1966, pp. 54–59.

140. I. F. Stone, "The Fatal Lure of World Domination," in Middleton, ed., *I. F. Stone's Weekly Reader*, 176.

141. Morgenthau, "Monuments," 8.

142. Christopher Lasch, *The New Radicalism in America, 1889–1963: The Intellectual as a Social Type* (New York, 1965), 331.

143. Kateb, "Kennedy as Statesman," 59–60.

144. Gore Vidal, "The Holy Family," *Esquire*, April 1967, p. 203.

145. William F. Buckley, Jr., "Gore Vidal on JFK," in William F. Buckley, Jr., *The Jeweler's Eye* (New York, 1968), 221.

146. Muggeridge, "Apotheosis of John F. Kennedy," 4.

147. Lasch, *New Radicalism*, 316.

148. Midge Decter, "Kennedyism," *Commentary*, Jan. 1970, pp. 22, 27. Decter reiterated these views in an essay review of Schlesinger's *Robert Kennedy and His Times*. Midge Decter, "Kennedyism Again," *Commentary*, Dec. 1978, pp. 23–29.

149. Henry Pachter, "JFK as Equestrian Statue: On Myth and Mythmakers," *Salmagundi* 1 (Spring 1966):5.

150. Henry Fairlie, "He Was a Man of Only One Season," *New York Times Magazine*, Nov. 21, 1965, pp. 129, 131.

151. Pachter, "JFK as Equestrian Statue," 7–8, 25.

152. Ibid., 26.

3. Kennedy Revised

1. Peter L. Berger, *Invitation to Sociology: A Humanistic Perspective* (Garden City, 1963), 57.

2. For the *Pentagon Papers'* revelations of Kennedy's role in increasing American involvement in Vietnam, see *The Pentagon Papers: The Defense*

Department History of United States Decision Making on Vietnam, Senator Gravel ed., 5 vols. (Boston, 1971), 2:1–276.

3. By contrast, some liberals and even radicals began to see distinct virtues in the supposedly somnambulent and provincial administration of Eisenhower. For a critical survey and analysis of the revisionist literature on Ike, see Richard Rovere, "Eisenhower Revisited—A Political Genius? A Brilliant Man?" *New York Times Magazine*, Feb. 7, 1971, pp. 14, 15, 54, 58–59, 62.

4. Of course, not all of the contributors to the revisionist reassessment of Kennedy were aligned with the New Left or shared exactly the same ideological presuppositions. Where possible, I have tried to suggest some of the variations in revisionist interpretations of Kennedy. It seems fair to say, however, that the great bulk of the revisionists were influenced by the critical perspective and spirit (if not the precise intellectual content) of New Left social science. For useful samplings and compendia of New Left thought, see Barton Bernstein, ed., *Towards a New Past: Dissenting Essays in American History* (New York, 1968); Paul Jacobs and Saul Landau, *The New Radicals* (New York, 1966); Walter LaFeber, *America, Russia, and the Cold War, 1945–1966* (New York, 1967); August Meier, ed., *The Transformation of Activism* (Chicago, 1970); Irwin Unger, ed., *Beyond Liberalism* (Lexington, Mass., 1971).

5. William L. O'Neill, *Coming Apart: An Informal History of America in the 1960's* (Chicago, 1971), 30; Ronald Steel, "The Kennedy Fantasy," *New York Review of Books*, Nov. 19, 1970, p. 3.

6. Bruce Miroff, *Pragmatic Illusions: The Presidential Politics of John F. Kennedy* (New York, 1976), 6; Steel, "Kennedy Fantasy," 10–12.

7. Richard J. Barnet, *The Roots of War* (New York, 1972), 140–48; Louise FitzSimons, *The Kennedy Doctrine* (New York, 1972), 8; Steel, "Kennedy Fantasy," 6; Ronald Steel, *Pax Americana* (New York, 1970), 340–41; William Appleman Williams, "Ol' Lyndon—and JFK," in *Some Presidents: Wilson to Nixon* (New York, 1972), 83–107.

8. Barnet, *Roots of War*, 109–10, 116–17; Miroff, *Pragmatic Illusions*, 12, 16; FitzSimons, *Kennedy Doctrine*, 13–15; O'Neill, *Coming Apart*, 23, 29–30; Steel "Kennedy Fantasy," 3–4, 8, 10; Richard J. Walton, *Cold War and Counterrevolution: The Foreign Policy of John F. Kennedy* (New York, 1972), chap. 1. For a good summary statement of the revisionist critique of the activist thrust of Kennedy's initiatives abroad, see Thomas G. Paterson, "Bearing the Burden: A Critical Look at JFK's Foreign Policy," *Virginia Quarterly Review* 54 (Spring 1978): 193–212.

9. FitzSimons, *Kennedy Doctrine*, 224–37; Miroff, *Pragmatic Illusions*, 39, 48–51.

10. FitzSimons, *Kennedy Doctrine*, 14, for example, praises Kennedy for his "superb" dealings with Third World leaders but concedes that they "were perhaps achievements of style rather than of substance." See also Miroff, *Pragmatic Illusions*, 110; and Walton, *Cold War*, 11, 203–207.

11. Walton, *Cold War*, 233.

12. FitzSimons, *Kennedy Doctrine*, 214. See also Barnet, *Roots of War*, 74–79; and Walton, *Cold War*, 171–74.

13. Richard Barnet, *Intervention and Revolution* (Cleveland, 1968), 157. See also David Horowitz, *The Free World Colossus*, rev. ed. (New York, 1971), 214–218, 230, 232, 412–23; Jerome Levinson and Juan de Onis, *The Alliance That Lost Its Way* (Chicago, 1970), 6, 35, 83–87; Miroff, *Pragmatic Illusions*, 113–31; and Steel, *Pax Americana*, 220.

14. Barnet, *Intervention and Revolution*, 158. See also Levinson and de Onis, *Alliance*, 85–86; Miroff, *Pragmatic Illusions*, 111–33; and Walton, *Cold War*, 207–15.

15. Steel, "Kennedy Fantasy," 8.

16. Barnet, *Intervention and Revolution*, 211; Steel, "Kennedy Fantasy," 8.

17. Barnet, *Intervention and Revolution*, 212. See also FitzSimons, *Kennedy Doctrine*, 70–71, 177–78, 186–87, 214, 226; Horowitz, *Free World Colossus*, 152–53, 424; Miroff, *Pragmatic Illusions*, 142–62; O'Neill, *Coming Apart*, 79–83; and Steel, *Pax Americana*, 340–41. For a useful survey of changing attitudes toward Kennedy and his Vietnam policies, see Kent M. Beck, "The Kennedy Image: Politics, Camelot, and Vietnam," *Wisconsin Magazine of History* 58 (Autumn 1974):45–55.

18. FitzSimons, *Kennedy Doctrine*, 33–71, 226; Walton, *Cold War*, chap. 3.

19. Edgar M. Bottome, *The Missile Gap: A Study in the Formulation of Military and Political Policy* (Rutherford, N.J., 1971), chap. 3; FitzSimons, *Kennedy Doctrine*, 88–124; Horowitz, *Free World Colossus*, 345–47, 358, 360–61, 366, 392–94; Miroff, *Pragmatic Illusions*, 68–82; O'Neill, *Coming Apart*, 31–33, 41–43; I. F. Stone, "Theater of Delusion," *New York Review of Books*, April 23, 1970, p. 20; Walton, *Cold War*, chaps. 4–5.

20. Barnet, *Roots of War*, 316; Barton Bernstein, "The Week We Almost Went to War," *Bulletin of the Atomic Scientists* 32 (Feb. 1976): 13–21; Bottome, *Missile Gap*, 91–92; FitzSimons, *Kennedy Doctrine*, 126–72; Horowitz, *Free World Colossus*, chap. 24; Miroff, *Pragmatic Illusions*, 71, 82–94; O'Neill, *Coming Apart*, 67–71; Ronald Steel, "End Game," *New York Review of Books*, March 13, 1969, pp. 15–17; Ronald Steel, "Cooling It," ibid., Oct. 19, 1972, pp. 45–46; Walton, *Cold War*, chap. 7.

21. Miroff, *Pragmatic Illusions*, 100; Steel, "Kennedy Fantasy," 8.

22. I. F. Stone, "The Test Ban Comedy," *New York Review of Books*, May 7, 1970, pp. 13–21. See also Bottome, *Missile Gap*, 97; FitzSimons, *Kennedy Doctrine*, 236–37; Horowitz, *Free World Colossus*, chap. 25; Ralph E. Lapp, *Arms beyond Doubt: The Tyranny of Weapons Technology* (New York, 1970), 20–21; O'Neill, *Coming Apart*, 87–88; and Walton, *Cold War*, chap. 8.

23. Miroff, *Pragmatic Illusions*, chap. 5; O'Neill, *Coming Apart*, 62–65. The revisionist critique of Kennedy's economic policies was largely anticipated in Bernard D. Nossiter, *The Mythmakers: An Essay on Power and Wealth* (Boston, 1964).

24. Miroff, *Pragmatic Illusions*, 223–33; O'Neill, *Coming Apart*, 14.

25. Miroff, *Pragmatic Illusions*, 233–70; O'Neill, *Coming Apart*, 73–75.

26. Marshall Windmuller, *The Peace Corps and Pax Americana* (Washington, 1970), 39–40, 48–50, 81–82.

27. O'Neill, *Coming Apart*, 49–53, 57–60; Hugo Young, Bryan Silcock, and Peter Dunn, *Journey to Tranquility* (Garden City, 1970).

28. See the remarks of Thomas Cronin quoted in Robert Reinhold, "Kennedy's Role in History: Some Doubts," *New York Times*, Nov. 22, 1973, p. 46. See also Steel, "Kennedy Fantasy," 11.

29. Hargrove is quoted in Reinhold, "Kennedy's Role in History," 46.

30. David Halberstam, *The Best and the Brightest* (New York, 1972), 19, 33, 51–53, 84, 125, 153–54.

31. Ibid., 86, 310, 366–68. For Halberstam on RFK, see his elegiac *The Unfinished Odyssey of Robert Kennedy* (New York, 1968). There are some

astute criticisms of *The Best and the Brightest* in Hanson W. Baldwin, "The Best and the Brightest?" *Intercollegiate Review* 9 (Winter 1973–74):43–44.

32. For some examples, see Barnet, *Roots of War*, 60, 74, 109, 146–48; Halberstam, *Best and the Brightest*, 125, 644–45; Miroff, *Pragmatic Illusions*, 15–17, 19; and Steel, "Kennedy Fantasy," 8. See also Noam Chomsky, *American Power and the New Mandarins* (New York, 1966). The "bureaucratic homicide" quotation is in Barnet, *Roots of War*, 16.

33. Nancy Gager Clinch, *The Kennedy Neurosis* (New York, 1973).

34. Ibid., 5, 6–7.

35. Ibid., 6, 13–14, chaps. 2–6.

36. See ibid., 33 ("may have been"), 36 ("may have driven"), 48 ("may well contain"), 57 ("could have"), 64 ("a logical guess is"), 101 ("strongly implies"), 102 ("can be"), 108 ("strongly suggests"; "it is not improbable"), 119 ("one suspects"), 208 ("strongly suggests"), 221 ("It seems evident"), 254 ("perhaps"). Characteristically, Clinch did not use such constructions to suggest the provisional nature of her argument, but to enlist the reader's assent to her more dubious assertions.

37. Ibid., 369, 372–73, 381–82.

38. Henry Fairlie, *The Kennedy Promise: The Politics of Expectation* (Garden City, 1973).

39. See Michael Oakeshott, *Rationalism in Politics* (New York, 1962). In a recent article, however, Fairlie has looked back wistfully at the activist civic *virtu* exhorted by Kennedy (while conceding some of the excesses to which it led) and deplored the gluttonous materialism supposedly prevailing in the age of Reagan. See Henry Fairlie, " 'Let the Word Go Forth': Citizen Kennedy," *New Republic*, Feb. 3, 1986, pp. 14, 16–17.

40. Fairlie, *Kennedy Promise*, 11, 186–87, 198, 206–207, 210–11, 215, 259. Typically, an American conservative, Robert D. Novak, denounced this book because of its reliance on left-wing revisionism. See Robert D. Novak, "Revisionism, Ltd.," *National Review*, March 2, 1973, pp. 269–70.

41. Fairlie, *Kennedy Promise*, 115–16.

42. Ibid., 289.

43. For some astute criticisms along these lines, see Arthur M. Schlesinger, Jr., "J.F.K.: Promise and Reality," *Commonweal*, May 25, 1973, pp. 291–92.

44. Fairlie, *Kennedy Promise*, 7–9, 28, 60.

45. Robert Patrick, *Kennedy's Children* (New York, 1976). In this play, a motley group of social outcasts in a nondescript bar lose themselves in autistic fantasies inspired by the social traumata of the so-called "sixties": the Kennedy assassination, Marilyn Monroe's suicide, Vietnam, drugs, racial strife, and promiscuous sex. "Wanda," a dowdy teacher of "subnormal" children, serves as the voice of Kennedyite idealism, but her inspirational clichés ring hollow against the backdrop of so much human wreckage.

46. Louis Harris, *The Anguish of Change* (New York, 1973), 201.

47. Gary M. Maranell, "The Evaluation of Presidents: An Extension of the Schlesinger Polls," *Journal of American History* 57 (June 1970):109–110. See also the views of James MacGregor Burns, Richard Neustadt, and J. David Barber quoted in Reinhold, "Kennedy's Role in History," 1, 46; and David Burner, "Kennedy: A Cold Warrior," in Robert D. Marcus and David Burner, eds., *America since 1945* (New York, 1972), 157–75.

48. Donald Freed and Mark Lane, *Executive Action* (New York, 1973).

49. Richard Condon, *Winter Kills* (New York, 1974). In this book, the

revisionist view of Kennedy is discredited by being put in the mouth of a bogus right-wing oil man. Ibid., 95–96.

50. The best recording of the *Mass*, conducted by Bernstein and with Alan Titus as the celebrant, is on Columbia Records (Columbia Label 231008). At the dramatic climax of this eclectic work, the chorus intones "Dona Nobis Pacem" ("Give Us Peace") as the celebrant goes mad, breaks the crucifix, despoils the altar, and strips himself of his vestments. At one point in the original performance, choirboys descended into the audience, pressed the flesh of members of the audience, and said, "Pass it on."

51. Richard Boeth, "JFK: Visions and Revisions," *Newsweek*, Nov. 19, 1973, p. 92; Anthony Lewis, "Time Remembered," *New York Times*, Nov. 22, 1973, p. 37; Andrew Greeley, "Leave John Kennedy in Peace," *Christian Century*, Nov. 21, 1973, p. 1150; Schlesinger, "J.F.K.," 293; Theodore C. Sorensen, "That Time We Huddled Together in Disbelief," *New York Times*, Nov. 22, 1973, p. 37; Tom Wicker, review of Fairlie, *Kennedy Promise*, in *New York Times Book Review*, Nov. 21, 1973, p. 1; Suzannah Lessard, "A New Look at John Kennedy," *Washington Monthly*, Oct. 1971, p. 10. See also Richard L. Strout, "Kennedy Legend—A View after 10 Years," *Christian Science Monitor*, Nov. 21, 1973, pp. 1–2; Joseph Kraft, "New Frontier Is 10 Years Old," *Los Angeles Times*, Jan. 17, 1971, p. G6; David Broder, "It Doesn't Seem Like Eight Years," ibid., Nov. 25, 1971, sec. 2, p. 7; Stuart Udall, "One of the Choice. . . , " ibid., Nov. 22, 1973, sec. 2, p. 7; and William V. Shannon, "J.F.K. in Retrospect," *New York Times*, Oct. 29, 1971, p. 43.

52. Abram Chayes, *The Cuban Missile Crisis* (New York, 1974), 94.

53. Robert M. Slusser, *The Berlin Crisis of 1961* (Baltimore, 1973), esp. x, 134, 149–51.

54. Arthur M. Schlesinger, Jr., *The Imperial Presidency* (Boston, 1973), 169, 173–76, 214, 215. Edwin C. Hargrove's supposedly "revisionist" book on the presidency has a similarly apologetic view of the Kennedy administration, premised on the notion of JFK's "growth" in his last year. See Erwin C. Hargrove, *The Power of the Modern Presidency* (New York, 1974), 64–69.

55. See chapter 5 of this work, "Kennedy on Balance."

56. O'Neill, *Coming Apart*, 75. Of the revisionists discussed in this work, only Miroff seems to have grasped some of the problems raised here. But his response (significantly relegated to a note) is far from satisfactory: "I do not mean to imply that Kennedy *should* have been expected to alter the political context in which he operated. The point of this discussion is not that Kennedy held attitudes on power that were extraordinary for an American political leader, but that he possessed a conception of power that was all too typical." Miroff, *Pragmatic Illusions*, 301n56.

57. O'Neill, however, has written perceptively on the unintended consequences of the Kennedy image itself: "Together the entire complex of attributes that made up the Kennedy image had an oddly liberating effect. A new order was struggling to be born; John F. Kennedy became its midwife. Such a thing cannot be proved. Perhaps American life in the sixties would have been much the same had Nixon been elected instead. No one believed this. President Kennedy's politics were hardly less conventional, and not much more liberal, than Nixon's. Yet he was, in Mailer's sense, an existential figure, and he opened the door through which all had to walk, however reluctantly." O'Neill, *Coming Apart*, 93.

58. On textbook views of Kennedy in the early 1970s, see John Berendt, "Ten Years Later: A Look at the Record. What the School Books Are Teach-

ing Our Kids about JFK," *Esquire*, Nov. 1973, pp. 140, 263–65. For examples of textbook interpretations of the Kennedy era influenced somewhat by revisionism, see Jim F. Heath, *Decade of Disillusionment: The Kennedy-Johnson Years* (Bloomington, 1975), chaps. 2–5; and Richard Hofstadter et al., *The Structure of American History*, 2d ed. (Englewood Cliffs, 1973), 387–400. For later views in a revisionist mold, see Allen J. Matusow, *The Unraveling of America: A History of Liberalism in the 1960s* (New York, 1984), chaps. 1–4; and Frederick F. Siegel, *Troubled Journey: From Pearl Harbor to Ronald Reagan* (New York, 1984), 123–51.

4. Kennedy Revealed

1. Theodore C. Sorensen, *Kennedy* (New York, 1965), 325. See also ibid., 322–30; Pierre Salinger, *With Kennedy* (Garden City, 1966), 54, 145; and Richard Schickel, *Intimate Strangers: The Culture of Celebrity* (Garden City, 1985), 165–86.

2. As Daniel J. Boorstin has written in *The Image: or, What Happened to the American Dream* (New York, 1962), 255, "The . . . quest for spontaneity helps explain . . . our morbid interest in private lives, in personal gossip, and in the sexual indiscretions of public figures. In a world where the public acts of politicians and celebrities become more and more contrived, we look ever more eagerly for happenings not brought into being for our benefit. We search for those areas of life which may have remained immune to the cancer of pseudo-eventfulness."

3. L. Smith, "Questions about Kennedy: Feedback between News and Newsmen," *Newsweek*, Aug. 4, 1969, p. 56; "Living with Whispers," *Time*, Aug. 22, 1969, pp. 13–14; "What Voters Think of Kennedy Now," *U.S. News and World Report*, Dec. 1, 1969, p. 16.

4. See, for example, Ray Hires, "The Secret Relationship between John F. Kennedy and Marilyn Monroe," *Midnight*, Dec. 20, 1971, pp. 1, 12.

5. Norman Mailer, *Marilyn: A Biography* (New York, 1974); Earl Wilson, *Show Business Laid Bare* (New York, 1974). Monroe's relationships with JFK and RFK will probably always remain mysterious, in good part because of inconsistent remarks by Monroe herself. According to Lena Pepitone, *Marilyn Monroe Confidential: An Intimate Personal Account* (New York, 1979), 237–39, Monroe "just laughed" at rumors that she was having an affair with either the president or the attorney general. W. J. Weatherby pointed to evidence of a possible affair with Robert Kennedy but claimed Monroe changed the subject whenever the topic of her relationship with JFK came up. W. J. Weatherby, *Conversations with Marilyn* (New York, 1976), 203, 206, 209, 213–14. Robert F. Slatzer quoted her as replying, "I'll never tell," when asked if she had an affair with JFK, but he suggested that she was murdered as part of a government cover-up. Robert F. Slatzer, *The Life and Curious Death of Marilyn Monroe* (New York, 1974), 24, 344–45. Tony Sciacca, *Who Killed Marilyn?* (New York, 1976), and Anthony Summers, *Goddess: The Secret Lives of Marilyn Monroe* (New York, 1985), claim that Monroe had affairs with both JFK and RFK; Sciacca also suggested that she was killed to cover up her involvements with the two brothers.

6. Bradlee, "He Had That Special Grace," *Newsweek*, Dec. 2, 1963, p. 38.

7. Taylor Branch, "The Ben Bradlee Tapes," *Harper's*, Oct. 1975, p. 36; Benjamin C. Bradlee, *Conversations with Kennedy* (New York, 1975), 10.

8. Bradlee, *Conversations*, 23–25, 116–17.

9. Ibid., 76, 227. See also ibid., 18, 76–77, 187.

10. Ibid., 33, 119, 166, 218, 148.

11. U.S. Congress, Senate, Select Committee to Study Governmental Operations with Respect to Intelligence Activities, *Alleged Assassination Plots Involving Foreign Leaders: An Interim Report . . . Together with Additional, Supplemental, and Separate Views, November 20 (Legislative Day, November 18) 1975* (Washington, 1975), 129, 129n2. The Church committee's findings had an interesting prehistory. Rumors of Kennedy-approved plots against Castro, which may have been encouraged by President Johnson as part of his feud with Robert Kennedy, circulated in Washington in the middle and late 1960s. Jack Anderson lent credibility to such stories in his column of March 3, 1967. After his retirement, LBJ himself suggested to Leo Janos that JFK was killed in retaliation for attempts to murder the Cuban dictator. The so-called "Rockefeller commission" investigated the alleged assassination schemes but found no conclusive evidence that JFK or RFK had approved them. See Seymour Hersh, "Aides Say Robert Kennedy Told of CIA Castro Plot," *New York Times*, March 10, 1975, pp. 1, 49; Leo Janos, "Last Days of the President," *Atlantic*, July 1973, p. 19; *Report to the President by the Commission on CIA Activities within the United States, Nelson A. Rockefeller, Chairman* (Washington, 1975).

12. Laurence Stern, "Probers Doubt Kennedy Knew of Poison Plot against Castro," *Washington Post*, Nov. 16, 1975, p. A6. This story revealed some of the Kennedy entourage's skill at concealment and euphemism. On the basis of information supplied by Evelyn Lincoln, Stern identified Campbell as a Kennedy campaign worker in California!

13. Victor Lasky, *It Didn't Start with Watergate* (New York, 1977), 16–20, 23–25, 83–104; William Safire, "Nixon Never Did," *New York Times*, June 5, 1975, p. 37; William Safire, "Murder Most Foul," ibid., Dec. 22, 1975, p. 29.

14. William Safire, "Put Your Dreams Away: The Sinatra Connection," *New York Times*, Jan. 5, 1976, p. 29; *idem*, "All in the Family," ibid., Jan. 26, 1976, p. 23; *idem*, "All in the Family: II," ibid., Jan. 29, 1976, p. 33; *idem*, "Frank and Jack and Sam and Judy," ibid., June 13, 1977, p. 29; *idem*, "J. Edgar's Private Files," ibid., Dec. 15, 1977, p. A20.

15. Nicholas Gage, "Questions Remain Despite Inquiries into Link of Kennedy Friend to Mafia," ibid., April 12, 1976, pp. 1, 26; *idem*, "2 Mafioso Linked to CIA Treated Leniently by U.S.," ibid., April 13, 1976, pp. 1, 22.

16. Peter Goldman et al., "A Shadow over Camelot," *Newsweek*, Dec. 29, 1979, pp. 14–16; "JFK and the Mobster's Moll," *Time*, Dec. 29, 1979, pp. 10–12.

17. Judith Exner with Ovid Demaris, *My Story* (New York, 1977), 103, 128, 148, 244. Some interesting information relating to the publication of this book appears in Margaret Montagno, "Memoirs: Lady in Waiting," *Newsweek*, Jan. 26, 1976, pp. 18–19; and "More Pillow Talk," ibid., March 1, 1976, p. 32.

18. The remark is in Arthur M. Schlesinger, Jr., "What the Thousand Days Wrought," *New Republic*, Nov. 21, 1983, p. 20. Some of the juicier stories about Kennedy's alleged sexual entanglements are in Stephen Dunleavy and Peter Brennan, *Those Wild, Wild Kennedy Boys!* (New York, 1976); Kitty Kelley, *Jackie Oh!* (Secaucus, N.J., 1978), 118–25, 130–31; Tony Sciacca, *Kennedy and His Women* (New York, 1976); Nelson Thompson, *The Dark Side of Camelot* (Chicago, 1976), chaps. 4–6; and Gene Tierney,

Self-Portrait (New York, 1979), 143. Such stories inspired a trashy *roman à clef*, Patrick Anderson's *The President's Mistress* (New York, 1976).

19. Traphes Bryant with Frances Spatz Leighton, *Dog Days at the White House: The Outrageous Memoirs of the Presidential Kennel Keeper* (New York, 1975), 22–24.

20. For versions of the Kennedy-Meyer affair, see "JFK's 2 Year White House Romance . . . Socialite Then Murdered and Diary Burned by CIA," *National Enquirer*, March 2, 1976, p. 1; Don Oberdorfer, "JFK Had Affair with D.C. Artist, Smoked 'Grass,' Paper Alleges," *Washington Post*, Feb. 23, 1976, pp. A1, A9; and Philip Nobile and Ron Rosenbaum, "The Curious Aftermath of JFK's Best and Brightest Affair," *New Times*, July 9, 1976, pp. 25–31. Characteristically, the *Post* tried to cast discredit on Truitt's story by pointing out that he had a history of mental problems.

21. Joan Blair and Clay Blair, Jr., *The Search for JFK* (New York, 1976), chaps. 5–6, 10–11, 15–18, pp. 583–84.

22. See Senate Select Committee, *Alleged Assassination Plots*, 139–46. The fullest account is in Taylor Branch and George Crile III, "The Kennedy Vendetta," *Harper's*, Aug. 1975, pp. 49–53, 56–63. Operation Mongoose was also the subject of a CBS documentary shown June 10, 1977, "The CIA's Secret War."

23. See, for example, the discussion of such matters in Herbert Parmet's two volume biography of Kennedy: *Jack: The Struggles of John F. Kennedy* (New York, 1980); and *JFK: The Presidency of John F. Kennedy* (New York, 1983). These books are discussed in chapter 6.

24. Peter Goldman, "Kennedy Remembered," *Newsweek*, Nov. 28, 1983, p. 64.

25. The blasé public reponse was noted in Lewis H. Lapham, "The King's Pleasure," *Harper's*, March 1976, p. 12; and Peter Steinfels, "The Kennedy Affair(s)," *Commonweal*, Jan. 30, 1976, p. 72. For a statement of such a view by a Catholic pluralist, see Albert J. Menendez, *John F. Kennedy: Catholic and Humanist* (Buffalo, n.d.), 80–81.

26. Lapham, "King's Pleasure," 13–14; Steinfels, "Kennedy Affair(s)," 72.

27. The press's change in attitude toward the Kennedys (particularly Edward) was noted in James MacGregor Burns, *Edward Kennedy and the Camelot Legacy* (New York, 1976), 273–74; Robert Sherill, *The Last Kennedy* (New York, 1976), 225–27; and Garry Wills, *The Kennedy Imprisonment: A Meditation on Power* (New York, 1983), 3–5.

28. Theodore H. White, *In Search of History: A Personal Adventure* (New York, 1978), 457, 529.

29. Arthur M. Schlesinger, Jr., *Robert Kennedy and His Times* (Boston, 1978), 494, 591.

30. Ibid., 485–89, 498, 538, 543, 549–50.

31. See Robert Sam Anson, *"They've Killed the President": The Search for the Murderers of John F. Kennedy* (New York, 1975); Brian K. Bugge, *The Mystique of Conspiracy: Oswald, Castro, and the CIA* (Staten Island, N.Y., 1978); Michael Canfield and Alan J. Weberman, *Coup d'état in America: The CIA and the Assassination of John F. Kennedy* (New York, 1975); Bernard Fensterwald, Jr., *Assassination of JFK: By Coincidence or Conspiracy?* (New York, 1977); Paul L. Hoch and Russell Stetler, *The Assassination: Dallas and Beyond—A Guide to Cover-Ups and Investigations* (New York, 1976); F. Peter Model and Robert J. Graden, *JFK: The Case for Conspiracy* (New

York, 1976); Carl Oglesby, *The Yankee and Cowboy War: Conspiracies from Dallas to Watergate* (Mission, Kan., 1976); David E. Scheim, *Contract on America: The Mafia Murders of John and Robert Kennedy* (Silver Spring, Md., 1983); Peter Dale Scott, *Crime and Cover-Up: The CIA, the Mafia, and the Dallas-Watergate Connection* (Berkeley, 1977); J. Gary Shaw and Larry R. Harris, *Cover-Up: The Governmental Conspiracy to Conceal the Facts about the Public Execution of John Kennedy* (Cleburne, Tex., 1976); and Anthony Summers, *Conspiracy* (New York, 1981). The assassination was also the subject of two major television programs: "The Trial of Lee Harvey Oswald," a four-hour miniseries broadcast on ABC September 30 and October 2, 1977; and "The Assassination of President Kennedy: What Do We Know Now That We Didn't Know Then?" a ninety-minute documentary produced by Witness Productions and Syndicast Services, in conjunction with the BBC.

32. *The Final Assassinations Report: Report of the Select Committee on Assassinations, U.S. House of Representatives* (New York, 1979), 31–336; "Who Killed JFK? (Latest Chapter)," *Newsweek*, May 24, 1982, p. 32. G. Robert Blakey, chief counsel and staff director of the committee, has published his own speculations on the assassination in a book coauthored by Richard N. Billings, *The Plot to Kill the President* (New York, 1981).

33. A 1983 *Washington Post*–ABC poll found that 80 percent of those questioned believed in the existence of a conspiracy, but 70 percent wanted no new investigation. *San Francisco Examiner and Chronicle*, Nov. 21, 1983, p. 1.

5. Kennedy on Balance

1. For descriptions of the dedication ceremonies, see Hank Klibanoff, "And Once Again, There was Camelot," *Boston Globe*, Oct. 21, 1979, p. 37; Martin F. Nolan, "A Day of Poetry, Politics, and Wit," ibid., pp. 1, 33–34; Eleanor Roberts, "The Beautiful Join the Best and Brightest," *Boston Herald-American*, Oct. 21, 1979, pp. A1, A3; Peggy Simpson, "Camelot at Columbia Point," ibid., pp. A1, A9; Terence Smith, "Carter and Kennedy Share Stage at Library Dedication," *New York Times*, Oct. 21, 1979, pp. 1, 31; and Peter Goldman, "Jimmy in Camelot," *Newsweek*, Oct. 29, 1979., pp. 32–34. On the night preceding the ceremonies, plans for the coming presidential campaign of Edward Kennedy were discussed at a private dinner party of key Kennedy advisers and friends. See William H. Honan, "The Kennedy Network," *New York Times Magazine*, Nov. 11, 1979, pp. 39, 114, 117, 132.

2. Gerry Nadel, "Johnny, When Will Ye Get Your Library?" *Esquire*, Jan. 1975, pp. 92–99, 130; *New York Times*, Nov. 25, 1975, p. 1.

3. Paul Goldberger, "A Sweeping Structure Symbolizes Years of Promise," *New York Times*, Oct. 21, 1979, p. 30; "A Concrete Memorial to Camelot," *Time*, Oct. 22, 1979, p. 63.

4. "Carter's Remarks," *Boston Globe*, Oct. 21, 1979, p. 2.

5. "Text of Senator Kennedy's Address," ibid.

6. This was the impression reported in James MacGregor Burns, *The Power to Lead: The Crisis of the American Presidency* (New York, 1984), 24.

7. Such a view is suggested by some of the voter opinions quoted in Steven V. Roberts, "Ted Kennedy," *New York Times Magazine*, Feb. 3, 1980, p. 64.

130 ■ Notes to pages 84–92

8. Peter Wyden, *Bay of Pigs: The Untold Story* (New York, 1979), 120–21, 264, 307–309, 313–26.

9. Desmond Ball, *Politics and Force Levels: The Strategic Missile Program of the Kennedy Administration* (Berkeley, 1981), xxi, 268–69, 277.

10. Michael Mandelbaum, *The Nuclear Question: The United States and Nuclear Weapons, 1946–1976* (New York, 1979), 7, 72, 76, 95, 133–37, 179.

11. Herbert S. Dinerstein, *The Making of a Missile Crisis, October 1962* (Baltimore, 1976), 2–3, 106, 131, 186–91, 230.

12. Ibid., 185, 188, 230, 234, 238. For a somewhat similar view, see David Detzer, *The Brink: Cuban Missile Crisis, 1962* (New York, 1979).

13. Weldon A. Brown, *Prelude to Disaster: The American Role in Vietnam, 1940–1963* (Port Washington, N.Y., 1975), 173–75; Leslie H. Gelb with Richard K. Betts, *The Irony of Vietnam: The System Worked* (Washington, 1979), 70–82; George C. Herring, *America's Longest War: The United States and Vietnam, 1950–1975* (New York, 1979), 74–75, 107; Paul M. Kattenburg, *The Vietnam Trauma in American Foreign Policy, 1945–75* (New York, 1980), 74, 96, 162–63, 190–92, 244; Guenter Lewy, *America in Vietnam* (New York, 1978), 418–23.

14. Gelb and Betts, *Irony of Vietnam*, 83–95, 279, 282–83; Herring, *America's Longest War*, 83–86, 94, 102–105; Kattenburg, *Vietnam Trauma*, 101, 108–10, 110–17; Lewy, *America in Vietnam*, 20–22.

15. Gelb and Betts, *Irony of Vietnam*, 90, 95, 191, 282–83; Herring, *America's Longest War*, 94, 107; Kattenburg, *Vietnam Trauma*, 113–16.

16. Carl M. Brauer, *John F. Kennedy and the Second Reconstruction* (New York, 1977), chaps. 1–8.

17. Ibid., 234–320.

18. Alan Shank, *Presidential Policy Leadership: Kennedy and Social Welfare* (Lanham, Md., 1980), chaps. 2–5, pp. 256–63.

19. Lewis J. Paper, *The Promise and the Performance: The Leadership of John F. Kennedy* (New York, 1975), 231–32, 242, 257, 318, 345, 366.

20. Harris Wofford, *Of Kennedys and Kings: Making Sense of the Sixties* (New York, 1980), 7, 360, 374, 175, 363, 456.

21. Ibid., 458–59.

22. For such a "balanced" textbook view of the Kennedy presidency, see the analysis by Robert Wiebe in Bernard Bailyn et al., *The Great Republic: A History of the American People* (Lexington, Mass., 1977), 1206–45. The woeful deficiencies of history texts are ably documented in Frances Fitzgerald, *America Revised: History Schoolbooks in the Twentieth Century* (Boston, 1979). Although it does not address directly the problem of the Kennedy "image," Morris Dickstein, *Gates of Eden: American Culture in the Sixties* (New York, 1977) does contribute to a fuller, more "balanced" view of the Kennedy era in American culture. Dickstein endorsed the common notion that the early sixties was basically an optimistic period, "with a scent of change in the air, a sense of things opening up, of new possibilities." But in some of the best fiction of the era, he also found "a secret history of the Kennedy years, when the terrifying specter of thermonuclear war flashed garishly one last time before beginning to dim, when fond hopes for building a better society were repeatedly mocked by our inability to deal with the society we have, when a President's civilized, cosmopolitan vision helped conceal the expansion of our imperial role." While the best books of the Kennedy years "partook of the imperial buoyancy" of the administration,

"their vision sometimes had a bleak, dead-end character that belied any official optimism." Ibid., 95, 120–21, 122.

6. Kennedy, Kennedy—and More Kennedy

1. David Alpern, "Drag on Teddy," *Newsweek*, Jan. 14, 1980, pp. 38–39; John Barron, "Chappaquiddick: The Still Unanswered Questions," *Readers' Digest*, Feb. 1980, pp. 65–72, 219ff; Ronnie Dugger, "Ganging Up on the Prince of Camelot," *Boston Globe*, June 29, 1980, p. 4A; William B. Furlong, "Chappaquiddick: Ten Years Later: The Torments of Teddy," *Saturday Evening Post*, July/Aug. 1979, pp. 38, 40, 42–44, 46, 50, 52–53; Susannah Lessard, "Kennedy's Women Problem . . . Women's Kennedy Problem," *Washington Monthly*, Dec. 1979, pp. 10–14; Steven V. Roberts, "Ted Kennedy: Haunted by the Past," *New York Times Magazine*, Feb. 3, 1980, pp. 54–56; "Night That Still Haunts Him," *Time*, Nov. 5, 1979, p. 22; "Sex and the Senior Senator," ibid., Nov. 12, 1979, p. 76; "Tide in Ted's Life," ibid., Jan. 28, 1980, pp. 28–29; Tom Shales, "Playing 'Get Teddy': The Anti-Kennedy Bias in TV News Reporting," *Washington Post*, Jan. 30, 1980, pp. B1, B11.

2. For the text of the speech, see *New York Times*, Aug. 13, 1980, p. B2. In his commentary for ABC News, the conservative columnist George Will pointed out the implicit anti-Carter message of this speech.

3. James MacGregor Burns, *Edward Kennedy and the Camelot Legacy* (New York, 1976), 88; Garry Wills, *The Kennedy Imprisonment: A Meditation on Power* (New York, 1983), 5; Roberts, "Ted Kennedy," 58, 64.

4. John Gregory Dunne, "Elephant Man," *New York Review of Books*, April 15, 1982, p. 10. This article is a sage review of Wills's *Kennedy Imprisonment*.

5. Of these, two were particularly noteworthy: Reg Gadney, *Kennedy* (New York, 1983), which appeared in conjunction with the NBC miniseries "Kennedy," included some of the revelations about Kennedy's private life (pp. 64–65, 124–25); and Jacques Lowe, *Kennedy: A Time Remembered* (New York, 1983), which was produced with the cooperation of the Kennedy family.

6. Frank Saunders with James Southwood, *Torn Lace Curtain* (New York, 1982), 8, 11.

7. Harrison Rainie and John Quinn, *Growing Up Kennedy: The Third Wave Comes of Age* (New York, 1983). The authors report that Ted "greatly helped" in writing the book and opened up some of the family files to them (p. 12). There was also a picture book on the younger generation produced with the cooperation of the Kennedys: Jeannie Sakol, *Kennedys: The New Generation* (New York, 1983). For an earlier, independently written account of the successes and travails of the younger Kennedys, see Bill Adler, *The Kennedy Children: Triumphs and Tragedies* (New York, 1980).

8. See Rainie and Quinn, *Growing Up Kennedy*, 187–91, 197–202, for the portraits of David Kennedy and RFK, Jr.

9. William Manchester, *One Brief Shining Moment: Remembering Kennedy* (Boston, 1983), esp. 12–13, 55, 201, 212, 215, 217–25, 273–77.

10. Ralph G. Martin, *A Hero for Our Time: An Intimate Story of the Kennedy Years* (New York, 1983), chaps. 3, 16, 22, pp. 143, 175, 368, 448, 485. Martin quotes Jacqueline as saying that she understood why JFK had lived life to the fullest, "And I'm glad he did." Ibid., 506.

11. Ibid., 135, 267, 320, 425, 449, 452, 452–53.

12. Herbert S. Parmet, *Jack: The Struggles of John F. Kennedy* (New York, 1980), 88–94, 97, 167–68, 172–75, 299–300, 310, 322–33, 396–97; Herbert S. Parmet, *JFK: The Presidency of John F. Kennedy* (New York, 1983), 117–20, 126–27, 158–59, 304–306. By his own admission, Parmet wrote these books to redress what he believed were imbalances in the previous assessments of Kennedy. Parmet has also confessed to having ambivalent (though largely favorable) views of JFK. See Walter Goodman, "Historians' Poll Ranks Kennedy High, but Authors Continue to Argue Case," *New York Times*, Nov. 21, 1983, p. B12.

13. Parmet, *JFK*, 351–55.

14. Wills, *Kennedy Imprisonment*, 5, 7, 9, 30–33, 84–123, 134–37, 143, 176–77.

15. Ibid., 28–37, chaps. 4–11.

16. Ibid., 152–53, 178, chap. 15.

17. Peter Collier and David Horowitz, *The Kennedys: An American Drama* (New York, 1984).

18. John H. Davis, *The Kennedys: Dynasty and Disaster, 1848–1983* (New York, 1984).

19. Collier and Horowitz, *Kennedys*, 18, 122, 129–31, 161–62, 174–76, 209, 283, 290–91, 305–309; Davis, *Kennedys*, 71–72, 92–93, 107, 128, 230, 237–39, 252–59, 274–80, 289–90, 317–78, 490–91, 519–20, 617–20. Another book in this genre has appeared recently, Doris Kearns Goodwin, *The Fitzgeralds and the Kennedys* (New York, 1987). However, as one might expect in a work by the wife of Richard Goodwin, it is pro-Kennedy in viewpoint.

20. Collier and Horowitz, *Kennedys*, 353–454.

21. Barry Bearak, "Kennedy: Lights Dim in Camelot," *Los Angeles Times*, Nov. 17, 1983, pp. 10–12; Ernest Conine, "Post-Kennedy Years—What If. . . ," ibid., Nov. 14, 1983, sec. 2, p. 5; Goodman, "Historians' Poll"; John Herbers, "After 20 Years, Kennedy Band Tends Legacy," *New York Times*, Nov. 19, 1983, pp. 1, 9; David B. Kaiser, "The Politician," *New Republic*, Nov. 21, 1983, pp. 15–17; Stanley Karnow, "No, He Wouldn't Have Spared Us Vietnam," *Washington Post*, Nov. 20, 1983, p. F1; Christopher Lasch, "The Life of Kennedy's Death," *Harper's*, Oct. 1983, pp. 32–40; Jerry Laws, "Kennedy Recalled as Symbol," *Houston Post*, Nov. 21, 1983, pp. 1A, 11A; William E. Leuchtenburg, "John F. Kennedy Twenty Years Later," *American Heritage*, Dec. 1983, pp. 51–59; Mary McGrory, "You Had to Be There to Know the Pain," *Washington Post*, Nov. 20, 1983, pp. F1, F4; Pierre Salinger, "If John F. Kennedy Had Lived," *San Francisco Examiner and Chronicle*, Nov. 22, 1983, p. 6; Arthur M. Schlesinger, Jr., "What the Thousand Days Wrought," *New Republic*, Nov. 21, 1983, pp. 20–25; Arthur M. Schlesinger, Jr., "JFK: What Was He Really Like?" *Ladies' Home Journal*, Nov. 1983, pp. 116, 168; Adam B. Ulam, "Lost Frontier," *New Republic*, Nov. 21, 1983, pp. 10–13; "A Great President? Experts Size Up JFK," *U.S. News and World Report*, Nov. 21, 1983, pp. 51–54; Tom Wicker, "Kennedy and Our Vanished Dreams," *New York Times Magazine*, Nov. 20, 1983, pp. 32–34, 59, 62. Kennedy was also the subject of several television programs, including "Kennedy," a seven-hour miniseries broadcast on NBC, November 20, 21, 22, 1983; "JFK," a two-hour documentary broadcast on ABC, November 20, 1983; and "Thank You, Mr. President: The Press Conferences of J.F.K.," broadcast on stations of the Public Broadcasting System. PBS also

rebroadcast the famous USIA documentary on Kennedy, "Years of Lightning/Day of Drums." For critical comments on such programs, see Henry Fairlie, "JFK's Television Presidency," *New Republic*, Dec. 26, 1983, pp. 11–13, 16.

22. Theodore H. White, *In Search of History: A Personal Adventure* (New York, 1978), 457. The disintegration of liberalism is an even more prominent theme in White's elegiac (and Kennedy-worshipping) *America in Search of Itself: The Making of the President, 1956–1980* (New York, 1982), esp. chap. 4, pp. 272–73.

23. Theodore C. Sorensen, "Complex Kennedy," *New York Times*, Nov. 22, 1983, p. A31. Significantly, the *New Republic*, whose recent editorial positions can be loosely classified as "neoliberal," has published largely favorable articles on JFK. See, for example, the *New Republic* articles by David B. Kaiser, Arthur M. Schlesinger, Jr., and Adam Ulam cited above in note 21. Although it is forgotten today, Kennedyesque "pragmatic" liberalism was sometimes described as neoliberalism in its own time. See, for example, Amitai Etzioni, "Neo-Liberalism—The Turn of the '60s," *Commentary*, Dec. 1960, pp. 473–79. For JFK's role as a model for contemporary neoliberals, see Randall Rothenberg, *The Neoliberals: Creating the New American Politics* (New York, 1984), 41, 44–45, 70–71, 128–29. For a scholarly view of JFK that may be loosely described as neoliberal, see David Burner and Thomas West, *The Torch Is Passed: The Kennedy Brothers and American Liberalism* (New York, 1984). See also Charles Peters and Philip Keisling, eds., *A New Road for America: The Neoliberal Movement* (Lanham, Md., 1985), 7, 17–18, 146–48.

24. For the poll's results, see Peter Goldman, "Kennedy Remembered," *Newsweek*, Nov. 28, 1983, p. 64.

25. This was noted in Michael Killian, "Are We a Nation of Imbeciles? Or Are Reagan and Carter That Great?" *Houston Post*, Nov. 29, 1983, p. B3.

26. Nancy Gager Clinch, *The Kennedy Neurosis* (New York, 1973), 2–3.

27. For John Glenn's attempts to tie himself to the JFK image during the 1984 primary races, see Elizabeth Drew, *Campaign Journal: The Political Events of 1983–1984* (New York, 1985), 179–80, 279.

28. Ibid., 35–36, 322–23, 328–29, 361–62, 366, 369, 376–78, 412; Peter Goldman et al., *The Quest for the Presidency, 1984* (New York, 1985), 87, 157, 236. Gary Hart's aping of Kennedy's mannerisms came so close to the verge of caricature that one of his advisers complained, "Gary overevokes the JFK image." Ibid., 87. Unsurprisingly, Kennedy became a favorite hobbyhorse of the candidates for the Democratic presidential nomination in 1988. See Robin Toner, "Far Trumpet Is Heard Anew as Candidates Invoke J.F.K.," *New York Times*, July 5, 1987, pp. 1, 14.

29. Drew, *Campaign Journal*, 595, 608, 668, 748; Goldman et al., *Quest*, 19, 379. For JFK's influence on one of the most important neoconservatives, Daniel Patrick Moynihan, see Peter Steinfels, *The Neoconservatives: The Men Who Are Changing America's Politics* (New York, 1979), 54.

30. See David Donald, "Getting Right with Lincoln," in David Donald, *Lincoln Reconsidered: Essays on the Civil War Era* (New York, 1961), 3–18; and Merrill Peterson, *The Jeffersonian Image in the American Mind* (New York, 1962).

31. See, for example, "Would FDR, Truman and JFK Vote for Reagan?" *New York Times*, Oct. 31, 1984, p. B6. This was an advertisement by liberal academics protesting Reagan's use of the names of Democratic presidents.

See also Drew, *Campaign Journal*, 686, 731, 749, for Mondale's protests of Reagan's political "grave-robbing." Ted Kennedy, of course, rejects the JFK-Reagan comparison. See Robert Scheer, "Ted Kennedy Cites Lasting Legacy of the New Frontier," *Los Angeles Times*, Nov. 21, 1983, pp. 21–22.

32. Reagan cited the Kennedy tax cut during the 1980 race as a precedent for the Kemp-Roth tax cut plan. See Elizabeth Drew, *Portrait of an Election: The 1980 Presidential Campaign* (New York, 1981), 113–14. Some of the similarities between Kennedy and Reagan (though not those emphasized here) are discussed in "Post Reporter: A Tale of Two Eras: Cold War I, II About to Collide," *Houston Post*, Nov. 19, 1983, pp. 1A, 27A.

7. Afterword

1. Attempts to plumb the (hypostasized) national unconscious have invariably yielded conclusions that are truistic, sophomoric, or projections of the psychohistorian's preconceptions. For some particularly egregious examples of such forays into collective psychoanalysis, see Lloyd DeMause, *Foundations of Psychohistory* (New York, 1982). On the general deficiencies of psychohistory (most of whose practitioners are more modest and sensible in their claims than DeMause and his followers), see Jacques Barzun, *Clio and the Doctors: Psycho-History, Quanto-History and History* (Chicago, 1974); and David E. Stannard, *Shrinking History: On Freud and the Failure of Psychohistory* (New York, 1980).

2. For the functions and nature of mass consumer images, see Daniel J. Boorstin, *The Image: or, What Happened to the American Dream* (New York, 1962); Stuart Ewen and Elizabeth Ewen, *Channels of Desire: Mass Images and the Shaping of American Consciousness* (New York, 1982); and Christopher Lasch, *The Minimal Self: Psychic Survival in Troubled Times* (New York, 1984), 19–20, 29–31.

3. Two recent books help in more clearly establishing the place of the Kennedy image in mass consumer culture. John Hellmann, *American Myth and the Legacy of Vietnam* (New York, 1986), 4, 36, 38, 71, 95, 108, 115, 121, 136–37, 166, 221, discusses the "Kennedy myth" in connection with views of the Vietnam War in the popular media, while the Kennedys' role in the "culture of celebrity" is examined in Richard Schickel, *Intimate Strangers: The Culture of Celebrity* (Garden City, 1985), esp. 165–86.

SELECTED BIBLIOGRAPHY

1. Newspapers and Periodicals

America
American Heritage
Antioch Review
Atlantic
Boston Globe
Boston Herald-American
Bulletin of the Atomic Scientists
Chicago Sun-Times
Chicago Tribune
Christian Century
Christian Science Monitor
Commentary
Commonweal
Current
Dallas Morning News
Des Moines Register
Detroit News
Ebony
Esquire
Harper's
Houston Post
Intercollegiate Review
Journal of American History
Ladies' Home Journal
Life
Look
Los Angeles Times
Nation

National Enquirer
National Review
New Leader
New Republic
Newsweek
New Times
New York Daily News
New York Herald-Tribune
New York Post
New York Review of Books
New York Times
New York Times Magazine
New Yorker
People
Political Science Quarterly
Progressive
Ramparts
Reader's Digest
Redbook
San Francisco Examiner and
  Chronicle
Saturday Evening Post
Time
U.S. News and World Report
Virginia Quarterly Review
Washington Monthly
Washington Post
Wisconsin Magazine of History

2. Books

Abel, Elie. *The Missiles of October: The Story of the Cuban Missile Crisis, 1962.* London: MacGibbon and Kee, 1969.

Adler, Bill. *The Kennedy Children: Triumphs and Tragedies.* New York: Franklin Watts, 1980.

Alleged Assassination Plots Involving Foreign Leaders: An Interim Report of the Select Committee to Study Governmental Operations with Respect to Intelligence Activities, United States Senate. Together with Additional, Supplemental, and Separate Views, November 20 (Legislative Day, November 18), 1975. Washington: U.S. Government Printing Office, 1975.

Anderson, Patrick. *The President's Mistress.* New York: Simon and Schuster, 1976.

Anson, Robert Sam. *"They've Killed the President": The Search for the Murderers of John F. Kennedy.* New York: Bantam Books, 1975.

Bailyn, Bernard; Davis, David Brion; Donald, David Herbert; Thomas, John L.; Wiebe, Robert H.; and Wood, Gordon S. *The Great Republic: A History of the American People.* Lexington, Mass.: D. C. Heath, 1977.

Ball, Desmond. *Politics and Force Levels: The Strategic Missile Program of the Kennedy Administration.* Berkeley: University of California Press, 1981.

Barber, James David. *The Presidential Character: Predicting Performance in the White House.* Englewood Cliffs, N.J.: Prentice-Hall, 1972.

Barnet, Richard J. *The Roots of War.* New York: Atheneum, 1972.

Bell, Daniel. *The Cultural Contradictions of Capitalism.* Paperback ed. New York: Basic Books, 1976.

Berger, Peter L. *Invitation to Sociology: A Humanistic Perspective.* Anchor Books ed. Garden City, N.Y.: Doubleday, 1963.

Blair, Joan, and Blair, Clay, Jr. *The Search for JFK.* New York: Berkeley Publishing Co., 1976.

Blum, John M.; Morgan, Edmund S.; Rose, Willie Lee; Schlesinger, Arthur M., Jr.; Stampp, Kenneth M.; Woodward, C. Vann. *The National Experience.* 5th ed. New York: Harcourt Brace Jovanovich, 1981.

Boorstin, Daniel J. *The Image: or, What Happened to the American Dream.* New York: Atheneum, 1962.

Bottome, Edgar M. *The Missile Gap: A Study in the Formulation of Military and Political Policy.* Rutherford, N.J.: Fairleigh Dickinson University Press, 1971.

Bourjaily, Vance. *The Man Who Knew Kennedy.* New York: Dial Press, 1967.

Bradlee, Benjamin C. *Conversations with Kennedy.* New York: W. W. Norton, 1975.

Brandon, Henry. *Anatomy of Error: The Inside Story of the Asian War on the Potomac, 1954–1969.* Boston: Gambit, 1969.

Brauer, Carl M. *John F. Kennedy and the Second Reconstruction.* New York: Columbia University Press, 1977.

Brown, Weldon A. *Prelude to Disaster: The American Role in Vietnam, 1940–1963.* Port Washington, N.Y.: Kennikat Press, 1975.

Bryant, Traphes, with Leighton, Frances Spatz. *Dog Days at the White House: The Outrageous Memoirs of the Presidential Kennel Keeper.* New York: Macmillan, 1975.

Buck, Pearl S. *The Kennedy Women: A Personal Appraisal.* New York: Cowles, 1970.

Buckley, William F. Jr., *The Jeweler's Eye.* New York: Putnam's, 1968.

Burner, David. "Kennedy: A Cold Warrior." In *America since 1945,* edited by Robert D. Marcus and David Burner, 157–75. New York: St. Martin's Press, 1972.

Burner, David, and West, Thomas. *The Torch Is Passed: The Kennedy Brothers and American Liberalism.* New York: Atheneum, 1984.

Burns, James MacGregor. *Edward Kennedy and the Camelot Legacy*. New York: W. W. Norton, 1976.

―――. *The Power to Lead: The Crisis of the American Presidency*. New York: Simon and Schuster, 1984.

Campbell, Joseph. *The Hero with a Thousand Faces*. 2d ed. Princeton: Princeton University Press, 1968.

Canfield, Michael, and Weberman, Alan J. *Coup d'état in America: The CIA and the Assassination of John F. Kennedy*. New York: Third Press, 1975.

Canterbery, E. Ray. *Economics on a New Frontier*. Belmont, Cal.: Wadsworth, 1968.

Chayes, Abram. *The Cuban Missile Crisis*. New York: Oxford University Press, 1974.

Chester, Lewis; Hodgson, Godfrey; and Page, Bruce. *An American Melodrama: The Presidential Campaign of 1968*. New York: Viking, 1969.

Clinch, Nancy Gager. *The Kennedy Neurosis*. New York: Grossett and Dunlap, 1973.

Collier, Peter, and Horowitz, David. *The Kennedys: An American Drama*. New York: Summit Books, 1984.

Condon, Richard. *Winter Kills*. New York: Dial Press, 1974.

Cooper, Chester L. *The Lost Crusade: America in Vietnam*. Greenwich, Conn.: Fawcett, 1972.

Corry, John. *The Manchester Affair*. New York: Putnam's, 1967.

Cousins, Norman. *The Improbable Triumvirate: John F. Kennedy, Pope John, Nikita Khrushchev*. New York: W. W. Norton, 1972.

Davis, John H. *The Kennedys: Dynasty and Disaster, 1848–1983*. New York: McGraw-Hill, 1984.

Degler, Carl N. *Affluence and Anxiety, 1945–Present*. [Glenview, Ill.]: Scott, Foresman, [1968].

Detzer, David. *The Brink: Cuban Missile Crisis, 1962*. New York: Thomas Y. Crowell, 1979.

Dickstein, Morris. *Gates of Eden: American Culture in the Sixties*. New York: Basic Books, 1977.

Dinerstein, Herbert S. *The Making of a Missile Crisis, October 1962*. Baltimore: Johns Hopkins University Press, 1976.

Dommen, Arthur J. *Conflict in Laos: The Politics of Neutralization*. Rev. ed. New York: Praeger, 1971.

Donald, Aida DiPace, ed. *John F. Kennedy and the New Frontier*. New York: Hill and Wang, 1966.

Donald, David. *Lincoln Reconsidered: Essays on the Civil War Era*. New York: Vintage Books, 1961.

Drew, Elizabeth. *Portrait of an Election: The 1980 Presidential Campaign*. New York: Simon and Schuster, 1981.

―――. *Campaign Journal: The Political Events of 1983–1984*. New York: Macmillan, 1985.

Ewen, Stuart, and Ewen, Elizabeth. *Channels of Desire: Mass Images and the Shaping of American Consciousness*. New York: McGraw-Hill, 1982.

Exner, Judith, with Demaris, Ovid. *My Story*. New York: Grove Press, 1977.

Fairlie, Henry. *The Kennedy Promise: The Politics of Expectation*. Garden City, N.Y.: Doubleday, 1973.

Fay, Paul B., Jr. *The Pleasure of His Company*. New York: Harper & Row, 1966.

Fensterwald, Bernard, Jr. *Assassination of JFK: By Coincidence or Conspiracy?* New York: Zebra Books, 1977.

Fischer, David Hackett. *Historians' Fallacies: Toward a Logic of Historical Thought*. Harper Torchbooks. New York: Harper & Row, 1970.

Fishwick, Marshall W. *American Heroes: Myth and Reality*. Washington: Public Affairs Press, 1954.

———. *The Hero, American Style*. New York: David McKay, 1969.

Fitzgerald, Frances. *Fire in the Lake*. New York: Vintage Books, 1972.

———. *America Revised: History Schoolbooks in the Twentieth Century*. Boston: Little, Brown, 1979.

FitzSimons, Louise. *The Kennedy Doctrine*. New York: Random House, 1972.

Fowler, Robert Booth. *Believing Skeptics: American Political Intellectuals, 1945–1964*. Westport, Conn.: Greenwood Press, 1978.

Freed, Donald, and Lane, Mark. *Executive Action*. New York: Dell, 1973.

Fuchs, Lawrence H. *John F. Kennedy and American Catholicism*. New York: Meredith Press, 1967.

Gadney, Reg. *Kennedy*. New York: Holt, Reinhart, and Winston, 1983.

Garrison, Jim. *A Heritage of Stone*. New York: Putnam's, 1970.

Garson, Barbara. *MacBird!* New York: Grove Press, 1966.

Gelb, Leslie, with Betts, Richard K. *The Irony of Vietnam: The System Worked*. Washington: Brookings Institution, 1979.

Germond, Jack W., and Witcover, Jules. *Blue Smoke and Mirrors: How Reagan Won and Why Carter Lost the Election of 1980*. New York: Viking, 1981.

Golden, Harry L. *Mr. Kennedy and the Negroes*. New York: World Publishing Co., 1964.

Goldman, Eric F. *The Tragedy of Lyndon Johnson*. New York: Alfred A. Knopf, 1969.

Goldman, Peter; Fuller, Tony; DeFrank, Thomas D.; Clift, Eleanor; Beachy, Lucille; Barnathan, Joyce; and Smith, Vern E. *The Quest for the Presidency, 1984*. New York: Bantam Books, 1985.

Goodwin, Richard N. *Triumph or Tragedy: Reflections on Vietnam*. New York: Random House, 1966.

Greenberg, Bradley S., and Parker, Edwin B., eds. *The Kennedy Assassination and the American Public: Social Communication in Crisis*. Stanford: Stanford University Press, 1965.

Guth, DeLloyd J., and Wrone, David R., comps. *The Assassination of John F. Kennedy: A Comprehensive Historical and Legal Bibliography, 1963–1979*. Westport, Conn.: Greenwood Press, 1980.

Guthman, Edwin. *We Band of Brothers*. New York: Harper & Row, 1971.

Halberstam, David. *The Unfinished Odyssey of Robert Kennedy*. New York: Random House, 1968.

———. *The Best and the Brightest*. Paperback ed. New York: Penguin Books, 1972.

Harris, Louis. *The Anguish of Change*. New York: W. W. Norton, 1973.

Harris, Seymour E. *Economics of the Kennedy Years and a Look Ahead*. New York: Harper & Row, 1964.

Heath, Jim F. *John F. Kennedy and the Business Community*. Chicago: University of Chicago Press, 1969.

———. *Decade of Disillusionment: The Kennedy-Johnson Years*. Bloomington: Indiana University Press, 1975.

Heller, Walter. *New Dimensions of Political Economy*. New York: W. W. Norton, 1967.

Hellmann, John. *American Myth and the Legacy of Vietnam.* New York: Columbia University Press, 1986.

Henderson, Bruce, and Summerlin, Sam. *1:33.* New York: Cowles, 1968.

Heren, Louis. *No Hail, No Farewell.* New York: Harper & Row, 1970.

Herring, George C. *America's Longest War: The United States and Vietnam, 1950–1975.* New York: John Wiley, 1979.

Hilsman, Roger. *To Move a Nation: The Politics of Foreign Policy in the Administration of John F. Kennedy.* Garden City, N.Y.: Doubleday, 1967.

Hoch, Paul L., and Stetler, Russell. *The Assassination: Dallas and Beyond— A Guide to Cover-Ups and Investigations.* New York: Vintage Books, 1976.

Hofstadter, Richard. *Anti-Intellectualism in American Life.* New York: Alfred A. Knopf, 1963.

Hofstadter, Richard; Miller, William; and Aaron, Daniel. *The Structure of American History.* 2d ed. Englewood Cliffs, N.J.: Prentice-Hall, 1973.

Karnow, Stanley. *Vietnam: A History.* New York: Viking, 1983.

Kattenburg, Paul M. *The Vietnam Trauma in American Foreign Policy, 1945–75.* New York: Transaction Books, 1980.

Kazan, Molly. *Kennedy.* New York: Stein & Day, 1964.

Kearns, Doris. *Lyndon Johnson and the American Dream.* Paperback ed. New York: New American Library, 1976.

Kelley, Kitty. *Jackie Oh!* Secaucus, N.J.: Lyle Stuart, 1978.

Kennedy, Robert F. *Thirteen Days: A Memoir of the Cuban Missile Crisis.* New York: W. W. Norton, 1971.

Kennedy, Rose Fitzgerald. *Times to Remember.* Garden City, N.Y.: Doubleday, 1974.

Kimball, Penn. *Bobby Kennedy and the New Politics.* Englewood Cliffs, N.J.: Prentice-Hall, 1968.

Klapp, Orrin E. *Heroes, Villains, and Fools: The Changing American Character.* Englewood Cliffs, N.J.: Prentice-Hall, 1962.

———. *Symbolic Leaders.* Chicago: Aldine, 1964.

Knapp, Daniel, and Polk, Kenneth. *Scouting the War on Poverty: Social Reform Politics in the Kennedy Administration.* Lexington, Mass.: D. C. Heath, 1971.

Koskoff, David E. *Joseph P. Kennedy: A Life and Times.* Englewood Cliffs, N.J.: Prentice-Hall, 1974.

Kraft, Joseph. *Profiles in Power: A Washington Insight.* New York: New American Library, 1966.

Lane, T. A. *The Leadership of President Kennedy.* Caldwell, Idaho: Caxton, 1964.

Lapp, Ralph E. *Arms beyond Doubt: The Tyranny of Weapons Technology.* New York: Cowles, 1970.

Lasch, Christopher. *The New Radicalism in America, 1889–1963: The Intellectual as a Social Type.* New York: Vintage Books, 1965.

———. *The Agony of the American Left.* New York: Vintage Books, 1969.

———. *The Culture of Narcissism: American Life in an Age of Diminishing Expectations.* New York: Warner Books, 1979.

———. *The Minimal Self: Psychic Survival in Troubled Times.* New York: W. W. Norton, 1984.

Lasky, Victor. *It Didn't Start with Watergate.* New York: Dial Press, 1977.

Latham, Earl, comp. *John F. Kennedy and Presidential Power.* Lexington, Mass.: D. C. Heath, 1972.

Lerner, Max. *Ted and the Kennedy Legend: A Study in Character and Destiny.* New York: St. Martin's Press, 1980.

Leuchtenburg, William E. *A Troubled Feast: American Society since 1945.* Boston: Little, Brown, 1973.

———. *In the Shadow of FDR: From Harry Truman to Ronald Reagan.* Ithaca, N.Y.: Cornell University Press, 1983.

Levinson, Jerome, and de Onis, Juan. *The Alliance That Lost Its Way.* Chicago: Quadrangle Books, 1970.

Lewis, Lloyd. *Myths after Lincoln.* New York: Harcourt, Brace, 1929.

Lewy, Guenter. *America in Vietnam.* New York: Oxford University Press, 1978.

Lincoln, Evelyn. *My Twelve Years with John F. Kennedy.* New York: David McKay, 1965.

———. *Kennedy and Johnson.* New York: Holt, Rinehart, and Winston, 1968.

Lippman, Theo, Jr. *Senator Ted Kennedy.* New York: W. W. Norton, 1976.

Longsdon, John M. *The Decision to Go to the Moon: Project Apollo and the National Interest.* Cambridge, Mass.: MIT Press, 1970.

Lord, Donald C. *John F. Kennedy: The Politics of Confrontation and Conciliation.* Woodbury, N.Y.: Barron's, 1977.

Lowe, Jacques. *Kennedy: A Time Remembered.* New York: Quartet/Visual Arts, 1983.

Lowi, Theodore C. *The End of Liberalism: Ideology, Policy, and the Crisis of Public Authority.* New York: W. W. Norton, 1969.

Mailer, Norman. *The Presidential Papers.* New York: Putnam's, 1963.

———. *The Idol and the Octopus.* New York: Dell, 1968.

———. *Marilyn: A Biography.* New York: Grossett and Dunlap, 1974.

Manchester, William. *Death of a President.* New York: Harper & Row, 1967.

———. *One Brief Shining Moment: Remembering Kennedy.* Boston: Little, Brown, 1983.

Matusow, Allen J. *The Unraveling of America: A History of Liberalism in the 1960s.* New York: Harper & Row, 1984.

Mayhew, Aubrey. *The World's Tribute to John F. Kennedy in Medallic Art.* New York: William Morrow, 1966.

Menendez, Albert J. *John F. Kennedy: Catholic and Humanist.* Buffalo: Prometheus Books, n.d.

Miroff, Bruce. *Pragmatic Illusions: The Presidential Politics of John F. Kennedy.* New York: David McKay, 1976.

Model, F. Peter, and Graden, Robert J. *JFK: The Case for Conspiracy.* New York: Manor Books, 1976.

Moral Crisis: The Case for Civil Rights, as Stated by John F. Kennedy [and others]. Minneapolis: Gilbert Publishing Co., 1964.

Morison, Samuel Eliot. *The Oxford History of the American People.* New York: Oxford University Press, 1965.

Morison, Samuel Eliot; Commager, Henry Steele; and Leuchtenburg, William E. *The Growth of the American Republic.* 6th ed. 2 vols. New York: Oxford University Press, 1969.

Morris, Charles R. *A Time of Passion: America, 1960–1980.* New York: Harper & Row, 1984.

Morton, Marian J. *The Terrors of Ideological Politics: Liberal Historians in a Conservative Mood.* Cleveland: The Press of Case Western Reserve University, 1972.

Murray, Norbert. *Legacy of an Assassination.* New York: Pro-People Press, 1964.

Navasky, Victor S. *Kennedy Justice.* New York: Atheneum, 1971.

Newcomb, Joan I. *John F. Kennedy: An Annotated Bibliography.* Metuchen, N.J.: Scarecrow Press, 1977.

Newfield, Jack. *Robert Kennedy: A Memoir.* New York: E. P. Dutton, 1969.

Nossiter, Bernard D. *The Mythmakers: An Essay on Power and Wealth.* Boston: Houghton Mifflin, 1964.

O'Brien, Lawrence F. *No Final Victories: A Life in Politics—From John F. Kennedy to Watergate.* Garden City, N.Y.: Doubleday, 1974.

O'Donnell, Kenneth P.; Powers, David F.; with Joe McCarthy. *"Johnny, We Hardly Knew Ye": Memories of John Fitzgerald Kennedy.* Paperback ed. Boston: Little, Brown, 1972.

Oglesby, Carl. *The Yankee and Cowboy War: Conspiracies from Dallas to Watergate.* Mission, Kan.: Sheed Andrews and McMeel, 1976.

O'Neill, William L. *Coming Apart: An Informal History of America in the 1960's.* Chicago: Quadrangle Books, 1971.

Paper, Lewis J. *The Promise and the Performance: The Leadership of John F. Kennedy.* New York: Crown, 1975.

Parmet, Herbert S. *Jack: The Struggles of John F. Kennedy.* New York: Dial Press, 1980.

———. *JFK: The Presidency of John F. Kennedy.* New York: Dial Press, 1983.

Patrick, Robert. *Kennedy's Children.* New York: Random House, 1976.

The Pentagon Papers: The Defense Department History of United States Decision Making on Vietnam. Senator Gravel ed. 5 vols. Boston: Beacon Press, 1971.

Pepitone, Lena, and Stadiem, William. *Marilyn Monroe Confidential: An Intimate Personal Account.* New York: Simon and Schuster, 1979.

Peterson, Merrill. *The Jeffersonian Image in the American Mind.* New York: Oxford University Press, 1962.

Plimpton, George, and Stein, Jean. *American Journey: The Times of Robert Kennedy.* New York: Harcourt Brace Jovanovich, 1970.

Powers, Thomas. *The Man Who Kept the Secrets: Richard Helms and the CIA.* New York: Alfred A. Knopf, 1979.

Raglan, Lord. *The Hero: A Study in Tradition, Myth and Drama.* Paperback ed. New York: Vintage Books, 1956.

Rainie, Harrison, and Quinn, John. *Growing Up Kennedy: The Third Wave Comes of Age.* New York: Putnam's, 1983.

Report to the President by the Commission on CIA Activities within the United States, Nelson A. Rockefeller, Chairman. Washington: U.S. Government Printing Office, 1975.

Roberts, Chalmers M. *The Nuclear Years: The Arms Race and Arms Control, 1945–1970.* New York: Praeger, 1970.

Rochette, Edward C. *The Medallic Portraits of John F. Kennedy (A Study of Kennediana). With Historical and Cultural Notes and a Descriptive Catalogue of the Coins, Medals, Tokens and Store Cards Struck in His Name.* Iola, Wis.: Krause Publications, 1966.

Ross, Douglas. *Robert F. Kennedy: Apostle of Change.* New York: Trident Press, 1968.

Rothenberg, Randall. *The Neoliberals: Creating the New American Politics.* New York: Simon and Schuster, 1984.

Rowen, Hobart. *The Free Enterprisers: Kennedy, Johnson, and the Business Establishment*. New York: Putnam's, 1964.

Ryan, Dorothy, and Ryan, Louis J., eds. *The Kennedy Family of Massachusetts: A Bibliography*. Westport, Conn.: Greenwood Press, 1981.

Sable, Martin H. *A Bio-Bibliography of the Kennedy Family*. Metuchen, N.J.: Scarecrow Press, 1969.

Sakol, Jeannie. Introduction by Kathleen Kennedy Townsend. Preface by Edward Kennedy. Photos by Frank Teti. *Kennedys: The New Generation*. New York: Delilah Books, 1983.

Salinger, Pierre. *With Kennedy*. Garden City, N.Y.: Doubleday, 1966.

Salinger, Pierre, and Vanocur, Sander, eds. *A Tribute to John F. Kennedy*. Chicago: Encyclopedia Britannica, 1964.

Saunders, Doris E., ed. *The Kennedy Years and the Negro: A Photographic Record*. New York: Johnson Publishing Co., 1964.

Saunders, Frank, with Southwood, James. *Torn Lace Curtain*. New York: Holt, Rinehart, and Winston, 1982.

Schachtman, Tom. *Decade of Shocks: Dallas to Watergate, 1963–1974*. New York: Poseidon Press, 1983.

Scheim, David E. *Contract on America: The Mafia Murders of John and Robert Kennedy*. Silver Spring, Md.: Argyle Press, 1983.

Schickel, Richard. *Intimate Strangers: The Culture of Celebrity*. Garden City, N.Y.: Doubleday, 1985.

Schlesinger, Arthur M., Jr. *A Thousand Days: John F. Kennedy in the White House*. Paperback ed. Greenwich, Conn.: Fawcett, 1965.

———. *The Bitter Heritage: Vietnam and American Democracy, 1941–1966*. Boston: Houghton Mifflin, 1966.

———. *Robert Kennedy and His Times*. Boston: Houghton Mifflin, 1978.

———. *The Imperial Presidency*. Boston: Houghton Mifflin, 1983.

Scott, Peter Dale. *Crime and Cover-Up: The CIA, the Mafia, and the Dallas-Watergate Connection*. Berkeley, Calif.: Westworks, 1977.

Shank, Alan. *Presidential Policy Leadership: Kennedy and Social Welfare*. Lanham, Md.: University Press of America, 1980.

Shannon, William V. *The Heir Apparent: Robert Kennedy and the Struggle for Power*. New York: Macmillan, 1967.

Shaw, J. Gary, and Harris, Larry R. *Cover-Up: The Governmental Conspiracy to Conceal the Facts about the Public Execution of John Kennedy*. Cleburne, Tex.: Shaw, 1976.

Shaw, Maud. *White House Nannie: My Years with Caroline and John Kennedy, Jr.* New York: New American Library, 1966.

Sherrill, Robert. *The Last Kennedy*. New York: Dial Press, 1976.

Siegel, Frederick F. *Troubled Journey: From Pearl Harbor to Ronald Reagan*. New York: Hill and Wang, 1984.

Slatzer, Robert F. *The Life and Curious Death of Marilyn Monroe*. New York: Pinnacle Books, 1974.

Slusser, Robert M. *The Berlin Crisis of 1961*. Baltimore: Johns Hopkins University Press, 1973.

Smith, Malcolm E. *Kennedy's 13 Great Mistakes in the White House*. New York: National Forum of America, 1968.

Sorensen, Theodore C. *Kennedy*. New York: Harper & Row, 1965.

———. *The Kennedy Legacy*. New York: Macmillan, 1969.

Steel, Ronald. *Pax Americana*. Rev. ed. New York: Viking, 1970.

Stone, I. F. *In a Time of Torment*. New York: Random House, 1967.

————. *The I. F. Stone Weekly Reader.* Edited by Neil Middleton. New York: Random House, 1973.

Stone, Ralph A., ed. *John F. Kennedy, 1917–1963: Chronology—Documents—Bibliographical Aids.* Dobbs Ferry, N.Y.: Oceana Publications, 1971.

Summers, Anthony. *Conspiracy.* New York: McGraw-Hill, 1981.

————. *Goddess: The Secret Lives of Marilyn Monroe.* New York: Macmillan, 1985.

Sundquist, James L. *Politics and Policy: The Eisenhower, Kennedy, Johnson Years.* Washington: Brookings Institution, 1968.

Thompson, Nelson. *The Dark Side of Camelot.* Paperback. Chicago: Playboy Press, 1976.

Thompson, William Clifton. *A Bibliography of Literature Relating to the Assassination of President John F. Kennedy.* San Antonio: Carleton Printing Co., 1968.

Tierney, Gene. *Self-Portrait.* New York: Wyden Books, 1979.

Toscano, Vincent L. *Since Dallas: Images of John F. Kennedy in Popular and Scholarly Literature, 1963–1973.* San Francisco: R & E Research Associates, 1978.

U.S. Congress. *Memorial Addresses in the Congress of the United States and Tributes in Eulogy of John Fitzgerald Kennedy, Late a President of the United States. . . .* Washington: U.S. Government Printing Office, 1964.

Walton, Richard J. *Cold War and Counterrevolution: The Foreign Policy of John F. Kennedy.* Paperback ed. New York: Penguin Books, 1972.

Ward, John William. "John F. Kennedy: The Meaning of Courage." In *Red, White, and Blue: Men, Books, and Ideas in American Culture,* 140–52. New York: Oxford University Press, 1969.

Weatherby, W. J. *Conversations with Marilyn.* New York: Mason/Charter, 1976.

Weisberg, Harold. *Whitewash.* Hyattstown, Md.: Privately printed, 1966.

Whalen, Richard J. *The Founding Father: The Story of Joseph P. Kennedy.* New York: New American Library, 1964.

White, Theodore H. *The Making of the President, 1964,* New York: Atheneum, 1965.

————. *The Making of the President, 1968.* New York: Atheneum, 1969.

————. *In Search of History: A Personal Adventure.* New York: Harper & Row, 1978.

————. *America in Search of Itself: The Making of the President, 1956–1980.* New York: Harper & Row, 1982.

Wicker, Tom. *Kennedy without Tears: The Man Beneath the Myth.* New York: William Morrow, 1964.

————. *JFK and LBJ: The Influence of Personality upon Politics.* New York: William Morrow, 1968.

Williams, William Appleman. "Ol' Lyndon—and JFK." In *Some Presidents: Wilson to Nixon,* 83–107. New York: The New York Review, 1972.

Wills, Garry. *Bare Ruined Choirs: Doubt, Prophecy, and Radical Religion.* Garden City, N.Y.: Doubleday, 1972.

————. *The Kennedy Imprisonment: A Meditation on Power.* Paperback ed. New York: Pocket Books, 1983.

Wilson, Earl. *Show Business Laid Bare.* New York: Putnam's, 1974.

Windmuller, Marshall. *The Peace Corps and Pax Americana.* Washington: Public Affairs Press, 1970.

Witcover, Jules. *85 Days: The Last Campaign of Robert Kennedy*. New York: Putnam's, 1969.

Wofford, Harris. *Of Kennedys and Kings: Making Sense of the Sixties*. New York: Farrar, Straus, Giroux, 1980.

Wolfenstein, Martha, and Kliman, Gilbert, eds. *Children and the Death of a President*. Garden City, N.Y.: Doubleday, 1965.

Wyden, Peter. *Bay of Pigs: The Untold Story*. New York: Simon and Schuster, 1979.

Young, Hugo; Silcock, Bryan; and Dunn, Peter. *Journey to Tranquility*. Garden City, N.Y.: Doubleday, 1970.

INDEX

"Abraham, Martin, and John": song by Dick Horder, 25

Alliance for Progress: pro-JFK explanation of, 30; revisionist critique of, 54

Alsop, Joseph: on JFK and Stevenson, 10; on JFK's style, 12

American University speech: Lasch's praise of, 47; Pachter's criticism of, 49

Anderson, Jack: column on anti-Castro plots, 127n11

Arthurian legend: JFK and, 120n132

Arvad, Inga: Blairs find evidence of affair with JFK, 75; Parmet substantiates affair, 96

Assassination of JFK: popular responses to, 2–3; conspiratorial explanations of, 22–23, 45

Ball, Desmond: discussion of his study of JFK arms buildup, 84–85

Barnet, Richard J.: on JFK's Latin American policies, 54; on counterinsurgency, 54–55; on JFK and Vietnam, 55

Bay of Pigs invasion: alleged role in JFK's growth, 21; Cuban exiles in as anti-JFK conspirators, 23; JFK's role in, 31; revisionist view of, 56; Wyden on, 84

Bell, Daniel: on middlebrow culture, 115n46; quotation of colleague, 120n132

Berger, Peter L.: on revisionism, 50

Berlin crisis: alleged role in JFK's growth, 31; explanation by O'Donnell and Powers of JFK's conduct during, 118n95

Bernstein, Leonard: his "Mass," 65, 125n50

Betancourt, Romulo: JFK's support of, 30

Blacks: response to assassination, 3; use of JFK as symbol, 8; view of JFK and LBJ, 25

Blair, Clay, Jr.: discussion of his and Joan Blair's *The Search for JFK*, 75

Blair, Joan: co-author of *The Search for JFK*, 75

Blakey, G. Robert: author of book on JFK assassination, 129n32

Boeth, Richard: praise of JFK, 65–66

Boorstin, Daniel J.: on interest in public figures' private lives, 126n2

Bosch, Juan: JFK's failure to prevent coup against, 54

Bourjaily, Vance: quotation on assassination from his *The Man Who Knew Kennedy*, 2–3

Bradlee, Benjamin C.: discussion of his *Conversations with Kennedy*, 71–72

Brandon, Henry: on JFK and LBJ Vietnam policies, 39

Brauer, Carl M.: discussion of his *John F. Kennedy and the Second Reconstruction*, 88–89

Buchan, James: JFK's favorite quotation from, 17; Fairlie and his influence on JFK, 64

Buckley, William F., Jr.: on Kennedys' role in American life, 47

Camelot: as image of JFK administration, 42–43; Lerner and Loewe musical, 120n127

Campbell, Judith. See Exner, Judith Campbell

Cape Canaveral: renamed for JFK, 4; restoration of original name, 110n11

Carleton, William G.: on JFK as folk hero, 41; critique of JFK's foreign policy, 45

Carter, James (Jimmy): encounter with Ted Kennedy at opening of Kennedy Memorial Library, 81–82; speech at library, 82; mentioned, 101

Castro, Fidel: and Alliance for Progress, 54; murder plots against, 73, 75; Dinerstein on motives in missile crisis, 85–86

Hackett, David: head of President's Council on Juvenile Delinquency, 18

Halberstam, David: JFK's attempt to remove from Vietnam, 17; on counterinsurgency and charisma, 37; discussion of his *The Best and the Brightest*, 60–61; comment of RFK to, 118n85

Hargrove, Edwin: on liberal view of presidency, 59–60; revisionist book on presidency, 125n54

Harkins, General Paul: mentioned, 36

Harris, Louis: on popular fears after assassination, 3; quotation of JFK on generations, 116n62

(Louis) Harris poll: 1973 survey indicates JFK's popularity, 65

Hart, Gary: Sorensen's support of, 100; unsuccessful presidential candidacy, 101; appeal to JFK image, 133n28

Heller, Walter: influence on JFK, 32

Hilsman, Roger: views on Vietnam in his *To Move a Nation*, 37–38

Hoover, J. Edgar: as JFK's antithesis, 18–19; possible influence over JFK, 96, 97

Horowitz, David: discussion of his and Peter Collier's *The Kennedys: An American Drama*, 98–99

Howe, Irving: early critique of JFK, 45

Humphrey, Hubert: use of JFK name in 1964, 112n6

Image: reasons for use of word, 4–5; role in "New Politics," 14; role in mass consumer culture, 106

Incomes policy: JFK's use of, 32

Jacobson, Max: Exner claim JFK received injections from, 74

Jagan, Dr. Cheddi: JFK role in destabilizing regime of, 54

John F. Kennedy Memorial Library: Kennedys' refusal of Fay's contribution to, 7; reasons for delay in construction of, 81; Carter–Ted Kennedy encounter at opening of, 82

John F. Kennedy School of Government (Harvard University): mentioned, 4

Johnson, Gerald: on JFK as hero, 41

Johnson, Lyndon B. (LBJ): hostile references to in Manchester's *Death of a President*, 7; uses of JFK's name, 8, 112n5; continuity of administration with JFK's, 22; relation to JFK image, 24–25; style of, 25–26; portrayals of relationship with JFK, 25–26; RFK's criticisms of, 27–28; early policies in

Vietnam, 36; and JFK plots against Castro, 127n11. *See also* Kennedy, Robert F.; Onassis, Jacqueline Kennedy; Vietnam war

Justice Department: civil rights policies under RFK, 33–34; revisionist criticism of policies under RFK, 58

Kateb, George: critique of JFK's foreign policies, 46; perception of JFK's growth, 47

Kearns, Doris. *See* Goodwin, Doris Kearns

Keating, Kenneth: RFK opposes for Senate, 6

Kemp-Roth tax cut: Reagan cites JFK tax cut as precedent for, 134n32

Kennedy, Caroline: informed by Maud Shaw of JFK's death, 7

Kennedy, David: drug overdose death of, 95

Kennedy, Edward M.: use of JFK's name, 6; and "Camelot," 77; and Chappaquiddick scandal, 77, 111n2; encounter with Carter at Kennedy Memorial Library, 81–82; 1980 presidential campaign of, 93–94; protest of Republicans' use of JFK's name, 134n32

Kennedy family: presence at JFK funeral, 3; attempts to shape JFK image, 6–8

Kennedy, Jacqueline. *See* Onassis, Jacqueline Kennedy

Kennedy, John F. (JFK): popularity, 1, 65, 100–101; assassination, 2–3; funeral, 3; tributes to, 3; "shrines" to, 3–4; groups using as symbol, 4; as man of reason, 8–12; style of, 12–15; character and personality, 16–17; youth and, 18–20; alleged growth of, 20–23; relations with LBJ and RFK, 26–28; achievements of, 28–34; views of policies in Vietnam, 34–41, 54–55, 86–88; as hero, 41–45; early critics of, 45–49; revisionist views of, 50–67; defense of by critics of revisionism, 65–67; on television, 70; revelations about in 1970s, 70–79; "balanced" views of, 83–92; diverse images of, 94–103, 105–6. *See also* Johnson, Lyndon B.; Kennedy, Joseph, Jr.; Kennedy, Joseph P., Sr.; Kennedy, Kathleen; Kennedy, Robert F.; Onassis, Jacqueline Kennedy

Kennedy, Joseph P., Jr. (Joe): alleged effect of death on JFK, 21